Ready or Not, You're a

Grandparent

Family
Eva

1459

Ready or Not, You're a

Grandparent

DEBRA EVANS

ChariotVICTOR
PUBLISHING
A DIVISION OF COOK COMMUNICATIONS

Victor Books is an imprint of ChariotVictor Publishing
Cook Communications, Colorado Springs, CO 80918
Cook Communications, Paris, Ontario
Kingsway Communications, Eastbourne, England

READY OR NOT YOU'RE A GRANDPARENT
© 1997 by Debra Evans

Cover design by Bill Grey
Cover photo by Helstrom Studios
First Printing, 1997
Printed in the United States of America
1 2 3 4 5 6 7 8 9 10 Printing/Year 01 00 99 98 97

Library of Congress Cataloging-in-Publication Data

Evans, Debra.
Ready or not, you're a grandparent/Debra Evans
    p. cm.
Includes bibliographical references (p.).
ISBN 0-7814-0244-1
1. Grandparenting. 2. Grandparent and child. 3. Grandparenting—Religious
aspects—Christianity. I. Title.
HQ759.9.E87   1997
306/874'5—dc21   97-12055
                                                        CIP

To the memory of Elizabeth Evans Gorman (1926–1994)

loving grandmother of

Joanna, Katherine, David, and Jonathan Evans

Nicole, Jess, and Amelia Vincent

Stella and Deena Evans

Micah, Laura, Andrea, Carla, and Mareah Beckwith

Also by Debra Evans

The Complete Book on Childbirth

The Mystery of Womanhood

Heart & Home

Fragrant Offerings

Beauty for Ashes

Without Moral Limits

Blessed Events

Preparing for Childbirth

The Woman's Complete Guide to Personal Health Care

Beauty and the Best

Christian Parenting Answers (General Editor)

Six Qualities of Women of Character

Kindred Hearts

The Christian Woman's Guide to Sexuality

Contents

GRANDPARENTING DURING PREGNANCY, CHILDBIRTH, AND NEW-BABY STAGES

———————————

BECOMING THE GRANDPARENT
YOUR KIDS WANT YOU TO BE

SHARING YOURSELF WITH YOUR GRANDCHILDREN

11 Leaving a Lasting Legacy

What do you want to leave your grandchildren? Here's a wealth of suggestions on how to create a lasting record of your family history and, even more importantly, how to give your grandchildren a spiritual legacy, nurturing their growing faith in God.

Preface

Becoming a grandparent, at least for me, was one of those once-in-a-lifetime experiences I will never forget.

My own mothering background includes four "natural" births—two in the hospital, two in our home—between 1972 and 1980. It was a time when women across America desired a return to traditional family-centered births, and I was no exception: I refused all pain medication during each labor, breastfed my babies immediately after their arrival, and wholeheartedly welcomed my husband's active participation at every stage. I assumed that when my daughters grew up and had babies, they would follow my enlightened example.

I was wrong, of course. When my oldest child, Joanna, gave birth for the first time, she had absolutely no interest in going through labor without an epidural block—the regional anesthetic that numbs a laboring mother from her navel to her toes. She wasn't entirely sure about breastfeeding, either—especially when complications with the baby meant that breast pumping would be required. "Wearing" her infant daughter in a cloth carrier, which I had personally and professionally advocated for over twenty years, was out of the question. Joanna was going to do it her way, just as I had done twenty years earlier. Like my mother, I found myself suddenly facing my daughter's elected birthing and mothering patterns with a certain amount of astonishment and curiousity. But most of all, I felt an almost over-whelming sense of pride in my daughter as she tentatively traversed today's maze of parenting practices. Now, three years later, as she prepares for her second child's birth, I look at her not only as my daughter, but as Abigail's mommy—a seasoned pro.

Having shared this, I would also like to tell you that I was ready to be a grandparent long before the event actually took place. Somewhere in my heart, I sensed that grandparenting would be a grand adventure. I even developed and taught grandparenting classes at St. Elizabeth Community Health Center in Lincoln, Nebraska, ten years *before* I became a grandparent myself! As a veteran childbirth educator, I enjoyed showing expectant grandparents "the ropes" at the hospital: the birthing room suites, the family-centered nursery, the comfortable lounges. We talked about the changes that had taken place in maternity care and parenting philosophy, the advantages of at-home recovery, the uniqueness of breast milk. It was a role I relished because I could easily imagine myself in my students' shoes. So, when the day eventually came when I could be a grandmother in earnest, you can probably picture the smile on my face when I saw Abigail for the first time. And I am still smiling.

Whether you are new to grandparenting or not, I think that you will find this to be an encouraging book, full of enthusiasm for one of life's greatest privileges—the privilege of being someone's grandparent. We have a unique part to play, you and I, in the lives of the little ones God sends to our children. Frankly, I believe our role is irreplacable! Who else but a grandparent, for example, will grin from ear to ear for twenty minutes just because a two-year-old mispronounces the word "spaghetti"? The joy we feel concerning our grandchildren is an incomparable phenomenon. But don't get me started, or I may end up making what is supposed to be a short preface into an entire volume on my granddaughter Abigail.

Enough already. It's time for you to get started reading. While most of the material in *Ready or Not, You're a Grandparent* is written for both grandmas and grandpas—parents of grown daughters and sons—much of the information (in the early chapters especially) concerns your relationship with the new mother. For simplicity's sake, I've referred to her as "daughter" and the new grandchild as "he." I'm counting on you to substitute "daughter-in-law" and feminine pronouns as needed. Underline to your heart's content, jotting down any thoughts you may have as you go along. It is my hope that you will find this handy manual a pleasant companion in the days and months ahead. May God be with you!

Debra Evans

1
Ready or Not,
You're a Grandparent!

"Mom . . . Dad . . . guess what? We're expecting a baby."

The news confirms it: a grandchild is on the way! And whether this is your first, second, or tenth grandchild, the announcement comes as a powerful reminder of the dynamic family bonds you share.

"When my daughter-in-law called to tell me the news, I was holding a cup of coffee," reports Janice. "Without looking, I went to set it on the table, but the table wasn't there. Bam! Down went the china mug. Up went the coffee."

Unlike Janice, Ed had been looking forward to becoming a grandparent for a number of years. "Being a dad, for me, was practice for being a granddad, though I'd never admit it to my kids," he says, grinning widely. "That's because my grandfather was my favorite person in the world while I was growing up—the only one who loved me unconditionally, no matter how mischievous I was! Now that my daughter is expecting a baby, I'm really looking forward to being able to just pour on the love."

For Sharon, the less-than-ideal circumstances surrounding her

> *There are three times when our lives are totally transformed by natural events without our having to say much about it: when we are born, when we die, and when we become grandparents.*
> Dr. Arthur Kornhaber, *Between Parents and Grandparents*

grandchild's conception did not dispel her inner excitement when her son's teenage girlfriend announced the pregnancy test's positive results. "I know they're going to face tough times, and I'm worried about that. But I also know that my grandchild deserves all the love and support I can give. It wouldn't make any sense for me to make things any more complicated or difficult than they already are."

> *By wisdom a house is built,*
> *And by understanding it is*
> *established; and by*
> *knowledge the rooms are*
> *filled with all precious and*
> *pleasant riches.*
> Proverbs 24:3, 4 NASB

What Janice, Ed, and Sharon discovered on the day they learned about their grandchildren's conception is that grandchildren do not come by our choice. Expecting a grandchild is about accepting new roles and responsibilities that arrive regardless of our advice or consent. Our grandchildren are given to us ready to be unconditionally nurtured, cuddled, and cared for. And opening our hearts to them changes us for the rest of our lives.

"Getting ready for grandparenting is entirely different from getting ready for parenting," explains Dr. Charmaine L. Ciardi. "There's no morning sickness or swollen feet, but there are changes. Our place in the family circle shifts, and subtle developments in our thoughts and attitudes are necessary to give birth to the grandparent in each of us."[1]

Grandparents in the Spotlight

Like most expectant grandparents today, you probably do not feel ready to sit quietly for hours in a rocking chair or on the front porch swing. As you look in the mirror, you may have a bit of difficulty calling yourself "Grandma" or "Grandpa," in spite of the new gray hairs you discover growing near your temples. Your life is busy, activity-filled, rewarding. Slowing down to savor the next generation may sound very appealing, yet you can't help but wonder: What will it be like to be a grandparent?

As our generation grows older, millions of us will be asking ourselves this key question. Perhaps this is why the grandparent role seems to be receiving more public attention than ever before.

Grandparenting classes abound around the country; magazines and newspaper articles feature prominent grandparenting stories; movies and television shows depict intergenerational family sagas; states pass laws ensuring grandparents' visitation rights after divorce.

But grandparents have always been special. Why all this fuss about a basic family tie that goes all the way back to Genesis?

"A new generation of elders is appearing in the 'advanced' countries of the world," explains Dr. Arthur Kornhaber in *Between Parents and Grandparents.* "The beneficiaries of social and medical progress, they are long-lived, healthy, educated, and more economically secure than at any other time in recorded history. Within a decade, their children will be grandparents. In the future, four-generation families will become more commonplace."[2]

For those of us who treasure our family relationships, this is truly good news. We look forward, with eager anticipation, to coming "full circle"—embracing a brand-new generation. We view grandparent status as a matchless reward for the long years of parenthood. We believe that becoming grandparents will open up a bright horizon of premium opportunities to us. And, upon hearing the mind-boggling news of our grandchild's conception, we already know in our hearts that the adventure is just starting.

"Simply becoming grandparents can open creative floodgates for elders to use the gift of time, health, and vitality, and gain the love and respect they deserve," Dr. Kornhaber asserts. "Also, it can earn them a vital place in the hearts of their loved ones and an important role in their communities. Shared with parents, the linchpin of the connection between grandparents and grandchildren, their role enriches all their lives and assures the continuity of the family. This is the greatest gift of all."[3]

What Only Grandparents Can Offer

Over the past decade, grandparents' involvement in providing effective birth and parenting support has significantly increased. As more couples realize the benefits of grandparenting to their children—

> *No one is born knowing how to be a grandparent. Suddenly we are thrust into that role, and what we do with it can be one of the most important contributions we make during the time the Lord gives us here on earth!*
> Dale Evans Rogers, *Grandparents Can*

and themselves—they are inviting their parents to play a more active part in their children's lives from the very first moments. They understand that the presence of caring, considerate grandparents adds a rich dimension to family life that simply cannot be achieved by any other means. The reasons for today's renewed interest in reviving the grandparent's role include these:

Grandparents function as a priceless family-life resource. Grandparents' gifts of time, love, wisdom, practical support, and perspective significantly enhance, enrich, and enlarge family bonds.

Grandparents create cherished opportunities for multigenerational get-togethers. Holiday traditions, birthday celebrations, memorable milestones, and other important events are passed from one generation to the next by grandparents.

Grandparents offer the calming reassurance of continuity. The kind of love and tender care grandparents offer supplies a soothing balm in a stressful world, demonstrating that the family is durable in times of change.

Grandparents provide a strong sense of history. Children learn about who their families are and where their families come from when grandparents share their stories, pictures, recipes, and memories with their family's latest additions.

Grandparents function as a back-up system in times of change and crisis. Families acutely appreciate knowing that there is "someone to fall back on" when exceptional events—such as childbirth, unemployment, sudden relocation, divorce, remarriage, serious illness, or death—occur.

Grandparents teach powerful truths about God. As grandparents' faith is lived out before an ever-watching younger generation, little ones see God's love displayed in many delightful forms.

"Becoming a grandparent is a deeply meaningful event in a person's life," confirm researchers Andrew J. Cherlin and Frank F. Furstenberg in *The New American Grandparent*. "Seeing the birth of grandchildren . . . is an affirmation of the value of one's life and, at the same time, a hedge against death. Grandchildren are also a great source of personal pleasure. Freed from the responsibilities of parenthood, grandparents can unabashedly enjoy their grandchildren."[4]

Thankfully, grandparents are waking up to the challenge of nurturing the next generation. Given current social challenges, our children and grandchildren appreciate our assistance. And, as Dr. Kornhaber reminds us, we have a higher level of education, better health, more resources, and a longer life expectancy than any previous generation has had.

It's a great time to be a grandparent!

Using This Book

Ready or Not, You're a Grandparent offers plenty of practical information to help you assume your unique place in the family. It will:

—affirm the indispensable role you play in your grandchildren's lives

—urge you to creatively adapt and share your family's favorite traditions

—suggest ideas for supporting your children in their parenting duties and responsibilities

—increase your understanding of current childbearing and infant feeding methods

—encourage you to share your distinctive Christian witness with your family

In upcoming chapters, you will discover a wide range of options to consider as you prepare to greet your grandchild and provide support to your children. Take what you need when you need it, discard whatever does not fit your own situation, and leave the rest for later.

Congratulations, Grandma and Grandpa! You have been given a blessed opportunity to pass on the best things life has to offer to the little ones who look to you for a special brand of love and affection. It is my hope that you will enjoy your grandparenting journey to the fullest in the years ahead.

Grandparenting During Pregnancy, Childbirth, and New-Baby Stages

2
Pregnancy and Childbirth Today

"When I had Darlene, I wasn't allowed to hold her until the day after she was born," a grandmother-to-be named Kathy told me at the end of a grandparenting class I was teaching. "I think it's wonderful that the policies have changed. But sending women home the day after delivery seems a little too much, doesn't it? I can't imagine what it would be like to go home less than twenty-four hours after the baby is born."

Overhearing Kathy's comments, another class participant chimed in. "But think about how expensive maternity care is now. If I remember correctly, my entire medical bill, including the doctor's fee, didn't exceed $1,000," said Susan, a fifty-seven-year-old high school teacher. "Today, it isn't unusual for the charges to reach five or six times that amount."

Susan's husband, Dan, nodded. "What really gets me, though, is that my son wants to be in the room when the baby's born. I still can't get used to the idea that he actually wants to help 'catch' Megan's baby. If I'd been in the room when Tom was born,

> *My frame was not hidden from you when I was made in the secret place. When I was woven together in the depths of the earth, your eyes saw my unformed body. All the days ordained for me were written in your book before one of them came to be.*
> Psalm 139:15, 16

23

I probably would have fainted."

As a childbirth educator, I have heard countless expectant grandparents make similar statements over the years. But it was only after I became a grandparent myself that I grasped the magnitude of what it means to support the choices one's child makes about childbirth and parenting.

Over the past fifty years, as expectant couples' reliance on professionals expanded, the role of grandparents constricted. Rapid, sweeping changes taught Americans to continually seek new and improved ways of doing things. As a result, by the time our children were born, we held little in common with our parents' childbearing experiences, just as they, in turn, had rejected many of their parents' birth and child-rearing practices.

Many grandparents-to-be are astonished by the tremendous changes in childbearing practices that have occurred over the past twenty-five years. Health care providers and hospitals have revised and redesigned their approach to maternity care; childbirth education classes are an expected part of couples' birth preparation; new mothers choose to breastfeed their babies in record-breaking numbers; hospital visitation policies have expanded to encourage grandparents' participation in birth and throughout the mother's recovery. Just as our childbearing experiences were not the same as those of our parents, we now find that our children's experiences differ considerably from our own.

New grandparents also find that the passing years have seen skyrocketing amounts of information concerning pregnancy and prenatal development. Chapters 2 through 6 will fill you in on concerns that may be of interest to you along the way. More detailed material is included under Additional Resources (page 181) for those who are interested. And of course, whole books are available on all of these subjects—see the list of recommended reading on page 210.

Pregnancy and Prenatal Development

Your grandchild's life began with the joining of two microscopic-size half cells, an ovum and a sperm. Each contained only half the number of chromosomes found in all other human cells. Once fused together, they became a single complete unit packed with all of the genetic information necessary for the baby's development. Like a scripted symphony, your grandchild's DNA code guided each growth phase, step by step; the cells rapidly divided at a mind-boggling pace, producing the uniquely differentiated structures that became the baby's skin, eyes, heart, ears, and toes.

"For you created my inmost being; you knit me together in my mother's womb. I praise you because I am fearfully and wonderfully made" (Psalm 139:13, 14). David's celebration song says it well: new life—the appearance of a brand-new person made by God—is a magnificently designed process.

Whatever the circumstances surrounding this little person's conception, there is no need to wait until the birth takes place to begin loving the baby as you love, support, and pray for his mother. As Mom's body, mind, and spirit are hit by pregnancy-induced hormone surges, heartburn, and hemorrhoids, she may appreciate an extra nutritional boost and a back rub. While both expectant parents will benefit from your caring nurture, your pregnant daughter especially deserves tactful pampering.

The normal and healthy state of pregnancy brings intense emotional and physical growth for an expectant mother; the baby's father experiences psychological change as well. As a couple, they have embarked on a journey that is not under their complete control. Questions loom large in their minds: Will the baby be okay? What will the labor be like? How is this pregnancy going to affect our relationship? Will my/her body still be appealing?

Do not be surprised if your children also start to scrutinize you. It is normal for expectant parents, especially first-time ones, to examine their feelings toward their parents. Do everything you can to promote family peace. Now is the time to affirm your children's adult status by loving them and letting go, by recognizing that they're free to determine their own parenting style. They will not be perfect parents. No one is.

FETAL DEVELOPMENT CHART

First month
- Egg is fertilized; embryo implants in uterine wall, reaches 1/4 inches in length
- Initial structures form: eyes, ears, mouth, umbilical cord, brain, spine, and spinal cord
- Simple digestive system develops
- Heart beats by the 25th day
- Arms and legs start to grow (26th to 28th day)

Second month
- Baby is 1 1/4 inches long, weighs almost 1/2 ounce
- Face appears; eyes look closed
- Tooth buds develop
- Internal organs, long bones, and fingers form
- Early blood circulation established

Third month
- Baby is almost 3 inches long, weighs about 1 1/2 ounces
- All main organs are formed—fetal development stage begins
- Fingerprints present; arms and legs move
- Human appearance; baby smiles and frowns
- Gender is distinguishable; baby urinates
- Heart beats 117 to 157 times per minute
- Ears completely formed by end of third month
- Baby flexes arms, kicks legs

Fourth month
- Baby is about 6 inches long, weighs 7 ounces
- Heartbeat strong; muscles vigorous
- Baby swallows and excretes amniotic fluid; sucks thumb
- Fingernails and toenails form
- Skin is transparent, thin; downy hair covers body
- Breathing movements begin: baby hiccups
- Placenta fully formed
- Baby fills uterine cavity

Fifth month
- Baby is 10 to 12 inches long; weighs 8 to 12 ounces
- Mother feels baby's movements

- Baby can hear and react to sound
- Hair, eyebrows, and eyelashes present
- Both sexes develop nipples, underlying milk-gland tissue

Sixth month
- Baby is 11 to 14 inches long, weighs between 1 1/2 to 2 pounds
- Eyes open
- Creamy, protective coating (vernix) covers wrinkled skin
- Strong hand grip present
- Baby's stool, called meconium, collects in bowel
- Heartbeat audible with regular stethoscope or ear held to mother's abdomen
- Baby may survive outside of womb with expert care

Seventh month
- Baby is 12 to 16 inches long, weighs 2 to 3 1/2 pounds
- Baby moves actively, continuously changes position
- Boy's testicles descend into scrotum
- Gains more than one pound
- Basic breathing movements present
- If born, baby has good chance of survival with expert care

Eighth month
- Baby is 16 to 19 inches long, weighs 3 to 6 1/2 pounds
- Baby is very responsive to sounds
- Sleep and wake cycles clearly felt by mother
- May "drop" into pelvis and assume birth position
- Lungs continue to mature
- Iron stored in liver
- Movements increasingly restricted as baby grows

Ninth month
- Baby is 19 to 21 inches long, weighs 6 to 9 pounds
- Baby continues to develop body fat, gain weight
- Downy hair covering almost disappears; skin less wrinkled
- Immunities pass from mother to baby
- Lung development completed
- Fingernails protrude beyond fingertips
- Arms and legs flexed
- Baby becomes less active
- Head circumference usually equals shoulder circumference

But they will learn from their mistakes. And, when requested, you can offer your help, support, and encouragement.

Supporting a Healthy Prenatal Environment

While in utero, your developing grandchild benefits from your support of a healthy prenatal environment. As the baby's organs undergo rapid growth, you will want to avoid exposing him to cigarette smoke. Your unborn grandchild's growth can also be promoted by not offering alcohol, caffeine-containing beverages and products, over-the-counter medications, and extra vitamin supplements to his mom. Avoid the use of toxic environmental agents, particularly herbicides and pesticides, in your home.

Your daughter will have a long list of substances to be avoided during her pregnancy, including some that probably never crossed your mind during your own childbearing years.

Expectant grandparents, just like expectant parents, can't help but wonder about the possibility of birth defects. Recent statistics look like this:

Of every 100 babies born in the United States, between 95 and 97 percent are born healthy and require no medical or surgical intervention. According to the March of Dimes Foundation:

—one of every 175 babies is born with a congenital heart defect

—one out of every 400 babies is born with a clubfoot

—one out of every 700 babies is born with a cleft lip and palate

—one out of every 800 babies is born with Down's syndrome

—one out of every 2,000 babies is born with spina bifida

To put these figures in perspective, consider this information also:

—twins occur in about one out of every 100 births

—triplets occur in about one out of every 8,000 births.[1]

A personal note: as the grand-mother of a child born with a

> *Birth is surrounded with mystery, and people fear what they don't understand. Women who know more about birth fear it less.*
> Dr. William and Martha Sears
> *The Birth Book*

major birth defect—spina bifida—I want to encourage you to trust God with your grandchild's well-being and development. Every child is uniquely created and loved by our heavenly Father, from Whom every good and perfect gift comes (James 1:17). I always believed this until Abigail arrived. Now, I know it.

Fifty Years' Changes in Childbirth: A Brief History

The twentieth century has brought many changes to childbirth practices, just as it has to every other aspect of our lives. Until the discovery of antiseptic techniques and anesthetics in the mid-1800s, childbearing was accomplished without them, and cross-infection was not uncommon. As a result, medical intervention became prevalent in the early 1900s, with women seeking hospital births in greater numbers with each passing year.

Women expected modern medicine to bring about a higher number of safe deliveries with less pain. But these changes in birthing practices didn't satisfy everyone. From the 1930s onward, starting with the publication of Dr. Grantly Dick-Read's thought-provoking book, *Childbirth Without Fear*, people began to speak out against the trend toward the "medicalization" of childbirth. A successful movement to return birth to the family, eventually encompassing many different views and organizations, was created. Here is a bird's-eye view of the history behind today's trends.

The Transitional Era: 1940-1965

In the post-war years, rapid change existed everywhere. Most American women enthusiastically welcomed modern concepts in maternity care when they were offered an alternative to the old-world birth practices of their mothers, grandmothers, and great-grandmothers.

With the emergence of obstetrics as a medical specialty in the United States, birth moved quickly out of the family's domain and into the hospital—and the transition happened in a hurry: in 1940, approximately 40 percent of all American births took place at home;

by 1965, the rate of hospital births was nearly 100 percent.[2]

Mechanical and medicinal intervention in birth immediately became commonplace. "What had begun in the 1920s as a pursuit of safety, comfort and efficiency, a shared effort by doctors and patients to have the 'best' for birth, had become by the 1950s and 1960s an unpleasant and alienating experience for many women," explain historians Richard and Dorothy Wertz. They add: "Hospital delivery had become for many a time for alienation—from the body, from family and friends, from the community, and even from life itself. The safe efficiencies had become a kind of industrial production far removed from the comforts of social childbirth or the sympathies of the proverbial doctor-patient relationship."[3]

Heavy sedation and lack of emotional support during labor, enemas, episiotomy (a surgical cut in the vagina), forceps delivery, and gas anesthesia for birth were routinely practiced. Moms and babies were separated after birth for twenty-fours or longer, then briefly reunited once every four hours; dads participated from a distance, unable to hold or touch their babies until after leaving the hospital; grandma and grandpa admired from afar, feeling hopelessly outdated. And at the end of a week-long hospital stay, the new family waved good-bye to the nurses and headed for home, after barely getting to know their new son or daughter.

I have seen many women in my grandparenting classes simultaneously marvel and grieve over their childbearing experiences when I explain today's birthing practices during the hospital tour. The ample-sized birthing rooms—comfortably decorated with soft lights, fully adjustable beds, Jacuzzi bathtubs, padded chairs, Impressionist artwork, wooden rocking chairs, and baby cribs—move them to rejoice for the opportunities their children will have, but also to remember what they lost.

Even though many expectant grandmothers are acquainted with family-centered maternity care through magazines and television dramas, seeing the difference between their birth experiences and the birth experiences of women today deeply stirs their emotions. One woman summed it up for everyone when she said, "I'm really glad my kids are able to have the kind of experience I wish I'd had. But it hurts me to think about what my husband and I missed."

Class participants have talked about enduring labor alone, without the benefit of caring companionship. Many tell me they received an amnesia-inducing drug, called "twilight sleep," that eerily numbed their emotions. Many share about missing the crowning achievement of their nine-month-long pregnancy—their baby's birth—when a whiff of gas, administered through a rubber mask, produced sudden unconsciousness. Some grandmothers-to-be become teary-eyed as they talk. Hearing them bravely recall their stories, I want to cry, too.

"We weep—those of us who were ripped from our unconscious mothers and were thrust into antiseptic steel cribs and hermetically sealed nurseries with a half-dozen other screaming babies who, like ourselves, were ripped from their comatose mothers," explains Christian professor Dr. Donald M. Joy, an experienced grandfather. "We weep at the deficit of attachment we have assumed was normal. We weep at the adversarial position we took against our parents without provocation. And those of us whose children were whisked away by a prophylactic nursing staff, to be returned to us often begrudgingly six hours later, may be inclined to mount an insurrection against the medical profession and the hospitals. . . .

> *The joys of parents are secret, and so are their griefs and fears.*
> Francis Bacon, *Of Parents and Children*

"But we were, all of us, part of a generation which picked up the tab on necessary, if humane, medical experimentation which, thankfully, is beginning now to return to us the opportunities for which humans were created."[4]

Though the wide availability of antibiotics and blood banks significantly reduced birth risks during the transitional era, modern childbirth methods introduced other kinds of physical and emotional trauma to the experience of childbearing. By the 1960s, women increasingly asked: Why are families separated during childbirth?

The Technological Era: 1965-1990

Unlike your mother, you may have taken childbirth preparation classes, given birth with your husband's assistance, and attended breastfeeding or postpartum support groups. Starting in the sixties, childbirth educators began to spread the good news: Childbirth isn't about suffering and forgetting, it's about actively participating in and remembering one of life's most incredible events! Factual findings in the late sixties and early seventies confirmed that confining healthy women to bed for birth and early postpartum interferes with labor and delays recovery. Unwilling to surrender childbirth to medical experts any longer, the real experts—mothers and fathers—brought birth back to the family.

Upon hearing about the way we were born, we took flight in the opposite direction, toward the days when our grandmothers birthed and breastfed their babies in a family-centered environment. After expressing our strong desire for better birth care, we promptly invited our husbands to our bedsides.

Most men welcomed the opportunity to experience childbirth alongside their wives and enlarged their definition of what "to father a child" means. As women learned new ways to strengthen their minds and bodies for giving birth, the term *mothering*, a verb used to describe a wide range of nurturing behaviors, appeared in people's vocabularies for the first time. The hallmarks of family-centered maternity care—birthing, breastfeeding, and bonding—soon became the norm.

Naturally, the breastfeeding rate soared. By the mid-1980s, for the first time since Grandma's generation, the majority of mothers breastfed their newborns, backed up by numerous scientific studies that evaluated breast milk's components through groundbreaking research. Test after test proved human milk is the ideal food for human babies. Lactation specialists, acquiring knowledge about breastfeeding through intensive study and firsthand experience, shared their skilled expertise with new breastfeeding mothers—yet another revival of an old maternity care tradition.

By 1990, hospital trends again shifted dramatically. Families increasingly stayed together in the same room for labor, delivery, recovery, and early postpartum. Women also left the hospital sooner, after just twelve to twenty-four hours, when high-cost hospital care was deemed unnecessary by insurance companies. The family's home environment—where foreign germs do not threaten Mom's and Baby's safety and hospital routines cannot disrupt sleeping and feeding patterns—became the primary place for healing after having a baby.

A number of modern birth practices remained open to question. Unlike in England and Western Europe, home birth and midwives in the United States were widely viewed as old-fashioned oddities—part of a distant past that few people had experienced. Though American hospitals were growing more "homelike," the use of advanced medical technologies and routine intervention in birth was still prevalent. Obstetricians, rather than family physicians and midwives, remained the top choice for uncomplicated pregnancy and labor; high episiotomy rates existed in spite of numerous research studies disproving the procedure's benefits; continuous electronic fetal monitoring became a standard practice; and the cesarean section rate grew by 500 percent, from less than 5 percent of births in 1970 to 25 percent in 1989.

Consequently, as the nineties approached, many people wondered how much medical intervention in birth is necessary and healthy. What are safe alternatives to expensive medical interventions? Can the cesarean rate be lowered safely? Who should attend the births of healthy laboring women?

The Information Era: 1990 and Beyond

With research teams studying American birth practices in virtually every university-affiliated hospital in the country, childbearing has now come full circle, from the simple birth settings of the early twentieth century, to the medically controlled deliveries of the mid-1900s, to watchful support of women's natural birthing abilities. Over and again, science has confirmed that God's good design for labor, birth, and breastfeeding cannot be duplicated mechanically. Women must feel safe, secure, and supported in order to labor normally.

For this reason, hospitals and maternity care staff are changing their practices to better provide for women's physical, emotional, social, and spiritual needs. Husbands, other siblings, and yes, grand-parents are common birth companions; midwives, professional labor support persons, and lactation consultants play an increasingly significant role in promoting healthy childbirth and breastfeeding; obstetricians and pediatric specialists stand by in a supervisory capacity, ready to step in as needed; hospitals advertise humane advances in competitive birthing center care; and medical companies continue to develop less invasive, more comfortable, high-tech equipment.

Cesarean rates are slowly dropping. Improved technology gives more information with less risk to mothers and babies. Shorter hospital stays deliver Mom and Baby back home within a day or less after the birth. Prenatal education, childbirth and parenting books and magazines, parents' support groups, and breastfeeding consultants play a major role in the learning-to-be-a-parent drama. With more birth alternatives available than ever before, educated parents are bringing birth back to where it belonged all along—to the family—by making informed choices in maternity care.

3
Greeting Your Grandchild at Birth

With the introduction of new childbirth methods and modern parenting techniques over the past fifty years, many grandparents feel awkward about assisting their children around the time of birth. But it doesn't have to be this way.

"The best day of my life was when my daughter was born," a woman was overheard saying in a restaurant. "But the day my grandchild was born—that was even better."

The birth of a grandchild is a brand-new beginning—an amazing marvel brimming with eternal significance. Diane, a fifty-two-year-old medical technologist, describes her reaction to the wonder of it all this way: "When our grandson, Jamie, was born, I didn't expect the surge of emotion I experienced. I felt such amazement, concern, anticipation, joy—and relief!

"Tears ran down my face as I tried to sit down, thinking I might topple over with excitement at any moment. Suddenly, time seemed to exist in two places. All at once, I pictured my daughter in my arms—the way she looked when I saw her the first time—and realized it was her turn to be the

> *May the Lord bless you from Zion all the days of your life; may you see the prosperity of Jerusalem, and may you live to see your children's children.*
> Psalm 128:5, 6

35

mother, that the baby in her arms was a part of me, but from a distance. There was this precious new person for me to love without having to carry the primary responsibility for his daily care, as I had done for my own children.

"Then Jamie looked up at me and I just started talking to him. He looked more like his father's family than our family—another surprise. I stroked his hair and told him how glad I was that he was born.

"Life had moved ahead, right before my eyes. A new generation had arrived. I was a grandmother!"

Former Denver Broncos coach Dan Reeves missed the birth of his eldest daughter while out on the road as a rookie with the Dallas Cowboys. But when his granddaughter, Caitlin, was born, he was right there in the birthing room, standing by.

"That was a miracle," says the muscular grandpa in his distinctive Georgia drawl. "It's hard to explain the feeling to see life. I didn't realize when they are born, how alive they are. She was so alive. She just came out of there kickin' and screamin' and yellin'."

Astonished that the hospital staff encouraged grandparents' participation, Reeves admits, "The biggest surprise of all is, I really had no idea it would be the tremendous thrill it is—one of the most exciting things that's ever happened to me. I would recommend it."[1]

Birth: A Family Event?

Over the years, I have been privileged to attend many births as a childbirth educator and labor partner. A handful of these were attended by the babies' grandmothers, and in one instance, the baby's grandmother and grandfather. Some people might consider this to be quite unusual, or even strange. It wasn't. In fact, for everyone present, it seemed perfectly ordinary—like the most natural thing in the world.

When a woman labors to bring forth a child, she must travel a road that has been negotiated many times before. Yet, for each woman, the journey is unique. As with other childbearing and parenting practices today, there's really no one "right" or "wrong" way to put together a family-centered birth experience: expectant parents do their best to figure it out as they go along.

A laboring woman is very sensitive to the people around her. Some women gain strength from their family's tender presence; other are inhibited by it.

Encourage your daughter and son-in-law to decide what's best for them. If they prefer to have you in the room for all or part of her labor, discuss everyone's expectations ahead of time. Does she want you to be an active labor partner, or simply be in the room? Are you comfortable with this request? How does your son-in-law feel about it?

In many instances, childbearing women today invite their mothers (and sometimes, their fathers) to share the baby's birth, but not the entire labor. If this is your daughter's preference, you may stay on-call at the hospital until she asks you to join her in the room. Many grandparents wait out the labor in hospital reception areas designed for this purpose.

"When you've seen a baby take its first breath, it's the beginning of a special bond," says La Leche League cofounder Marian Tompson, who has attended nearly all her grandchildren's births. "It certainly is different than hearing the baby was born."

Though a seasoned pro, Marian considers herself a "typical grandmother," giving the kind of care grandmothers give best. "I wanted to help my daughters and their husbands through labor. No matter how prepared a woman is, she needs someone to help her tune in with what's happening—loving people to reassure her and tell her she's doing fine."

Marian describes her participation in her five daughters' labors as "an emotionally nourishing experience—[it was] an atmosphere laden with love." She believes that grandparent-attended childbirth is a growing phenomenon that demonstrates a family's desire to stay together, closing both the geographical and emotional gaps created during the past few decades.

"Grandparenting becomes what it should be," she says, "the next

> *Make no mistake about it, responsibilities toward other human beings are the greatest blessings God can send us.*
> Dorothy Dix

LABOR & BIRTH PREVIEW

Even if you will not be participating in your daughter's labor
and delivery, you may benefit from reviewing the stages involved.

EVENTS	EMOTIONS
Stage 1: Opening of the cervix	
Uterus contracts	Early labor: Excitement, anxiety, concern
Cervix effaces and dilates (thins, opens)	Active labor: coping-oriented, task-centered
Baby moves deeper into pelvis	Transition: introspective, withdrawn, discouraged
Stage 2: Movement of baby through the birth canal	
Uterus contracts and pushes	Complete concentration and involvement
Baby passes through pelvis	Disbelief that pressure is baby's head
Birth	Joy, relief, concern for baby's well-being
Stage 3: Expulsion of the placenta	
Uterus contracts	Awe, exhilaration, amazement; wondering about baby
Placenta detaches, leaves body	Irritability about post-birth care, afterbirth contractions
Stage 4: Two-hour recovery period after childbirth	
Uterus contracts ("afterpains")	Emotionally sensitive, reflective, aware
Healing process begins	Desire for comfort and quiet
Hormone drop initiates lactation	Open to bonding with baby

Stage 5: Six-week recovery period after childbirth

Uterus contracts, returns to earlier size	Wide range of emotions possible: happiness,
Lactation is established through nursing	anger, ambivalence, frustration, amazement,
If not nursing, breasts return to normal	sadness, gratitude, fear, appreciation, anxiety

generation coming into the world and being very much a part of your life."[2]

Participating in a loved one's labor and birth is an exhilarating, exhausting, anxiety-producing, awe-inspiring experience. Something very special happens in the room when a baby emerges from the womb. Perhaps it's because, no matter how much we try to factually comprehend it, birth is also a spiritual event, a passing of life from the Creator's hand to the family's heart.

Caring and competent labor companions provide a welcome, comforting point of reference. If you are invited to provide this kind of assistance during your grandchild's birth, you can find more information about what it means to be a labor partner and useful suggestions for increasing the grandparents' role during childbearing in the Additional Resources, pages 181-188.

If your children do not ask for your help, or you prefer not to participate in your grandchild's birth, think about alternative ways to convey your love and concern. You can offer prayer support, make time for regular phone updates, and give postpartum assistance.

Distance or family tensions may prevent your attendance at the birth. Anne and James Davis live almost two thousand miles away from their daughter's family, but that didn't prevent them from witnessing their grandchildren's births. "We decided our help would be more valuable *after* each of the babies arrived. Also, there wasn't any way to predict the timing of Judy's labor, so we couldn't schedule advance-purchase plane reservations," shares Anne.

"After Jimmy, our first grandchild, was born, Judy sent us a videotape of the delivery—the next best thing to actually being there. James and I were thrilled! Tears started streaming down our faces. We watched the tape over and over. And when we finally were introduced to Jimmy in person, we felt as if we had already met.

"Our second grandchild, Travis, was born two months ago," Anne told me recently. "Once again, Judy sent us a tape, and when we saw it, James and I just sat and wept. I can't tell you how much it means to us for Judy to have included us in the boys' births."

Becoming Acquainted

The birth of a grandchild is an astonishing, unforgettable event. You can expect to remember your first impressions of the baby (and details of the birth, if you were there) as you recall these moments in the years ahead.

Soon after the baby arrives, you may have the opportunity to hold your grandchild if no unusual health conditions exist. Notice how alert and quiet the baby is. Once he makes the initial adjustment to life outside the womb, he will spend several hours learning about his new environment. It's an ideal time for becoming acquainted.

Babies are born with an amazing array of social skills. They arrive well-prepared to form family attachments. Research studies have consistently demonstrated that newborns prefer human faces to other objects, recognize familiar voices, respond to the smell of their own mother's milk, and thrive upon cuddling and stroking.

You will want to be thoughtful about supporting the mother and father as they meet their baby, waiting to take your turn until they suggest you hold the baby. Don't be surprised if, once you are given the opportunity, you want to sit and gaze for as long as possible at your grandchild. Remember: birth is a spiritually sensitive time. However much we may try to think in rational, scientific terms about it, we are humbled by the mysterious awareness that another human being has joined the family circle, a child given life by the almighty Giver of life.

The sights, smells, and sounds associated with this newborn will become deeply imprinted on your memory—a precious gift from the Creator who has designed both of you for a two-way relationship, beginning at birth. In the hours and days following the baby's arrival, enjoy your grandchild's ready-made ability to make human attachments through:

Sight. Babies are equipped with a "zoom lens" ability to focus their eyes in the first few hours after birth. After this time, the baby's vision tends to become fixed at a focal length of about ten to twelve inches. (Not surprisingly, this is also the distance between the baby's face and mother's face during breastfeeding.) Though the "zoom" response fades temporarily, it reappears several weeks after the baby is born. Holding the baby in your arms will maximize your grandchild's ability to visually bond with you.

Sound. Babies respond best to high-pitched, elevated vocal and music sounds (Vivaldi's "The Four Seasons" is a proven favorite). Cooing and singing are good ways to introduce yourself to your grandchild. Watch as he follows your voice and reacts with his body to the rise and fall of your voice.

Touch. As the largest organ of the human body, our skin contains remarkable sensory capabilities. Skin-to-skin contact with newborns powerfully affects bonding and attachment

Smell. Think back on your earliest parenting experiences with a newborn, and you're likely to instantly recall the sweet-smelling aroma of your infant's hair or the delicate odor of her skin. This "baby smell" enhanced your desire to hold, cradle, and embrace your baby. As you hold your grandchild, you will more than likely find the unique fragrances of infancy irresistible once again.

Eye contact, hearing, touch, and smell are key components of early human interaction that help children acquire the ability to love and care for others. As your grandchild's senses come

> *In the sheltered simplicity of the first days after a baby is born, one sees again the magical closed circle, the miraculous sense of two people existing only for each other.*
> Anne Morrow Lindbergh, *Gift from the Sea*

into contact with your body and he experiences communication with you through your eyes, facial expressions, sounds you make, and snuggles you give him, a mutually beneficial attachment takes place. It's a back-and-forth process: I look at you, you look back at me; I speak, you wiggle and smile; I touch you, you get to know me; I respond to your cries, you discover you can trust me to meet your needs. This spectacularly choreographed set of exchanges helps to creates a durable bond between family members.

Although the baby will primarily be held and comforted by his parents during this time, your presence will provide an extra set of welcoming arms when his mom and dad need to take breaks.

Have fun!

Unexpected Outcomes

With many factors interacting to make each labor and birth unique, it's impossible to predict what will take place in any given situation. Unexpected events often happen.

During childbearing, challenging circumstances are not unusual—from going two weeks past the due date (when the doctor predicted the baby's early arrival) to having twins (when just one baby was anticipated) to having a long labor. At times, more serious complications involving the mother and/or baby occur.

If something unexpected takes place during your grandchild's birth:

Give your fear to God. Pray for the baby and the parents, recalling specific Bible promises.

Stay calm. Ask God to sustain you by His strength as you face feelings of disappointment, helplessness, anger, fear, sadness, or loss.

Accept your feelings. Don't be ashamed of the way you feel. Realize that loss brings grief—a process marked by a diverse array of emotions, including disbelief, denial, sorrow, loneliness, anger, irritability, restlessness, disorganized thinking, fantasy, and physical stress manifestations.

Get accurate information. Don't hesitate to ask questions. Be involved in what's going on so that you can better understand how you can help, what can be done, and what the true outlook is.

Pray for the medical staff. Pray that the Lord will guide the hands, thoughts, and decisions of the medical staff caring for your daughter and grandchild.

After the unexpected event:

Remember that others have experienced similar situations—you are not alone. Other families have also faced a situation similar to yours, many of whom are willing to offer support and information. Avoid isolating yourself from their assistance. Ask for a referral from the medical staff or your pastor.

Allow time to heal your hurt. Whenever loss is experienced, whether the loss of a dream or the loss of a life, emotional hurt is produced. Such wounds cannot be healed by doctors. Only God, through the Holy Spirit, time, and the help of capable and caring people, can ultimately bring healing in this area.

Avoid making comparisons. Try not to compare your situation to what is considered "normal." Be attentive to what God would have you learn by spending time quietly waiting in his presence.

Seek pastoral and professional support as needed. Ask for help if it isn't offered. Even strong, resilient people benefit from being able to talk about their unexpected birth outcomes.

Try to get adequate rest and avoid stress-aggravating substances. It isn't possible to feel clearheaded if the body's need for sleep and nutrients is neglected. Avoid excessive amounts of caffeine (coffee, tea, soft drinks), MSG, nicotine, and sugary foods, which promote nervousness. Drink water, herbal teas, and fruit juice; regularly eat nourishing foods.

Make peace with God. You may never know why things happened as they did. Accept that God heard your prayers, knew your desires and expectations, and answered them in this way for reasons only He can understand. Be honest with your feelings, presenting them to God and allowing Him to help you face your emotions one day at a time.

4
What New Parents Need (and Want)

After their baby's birth, the new parents receive constant care from a well-trained maternity support staff. With one push of the call button, help is readily available. Meals, medications, pitchers of ice water, pediatric advice, breastfeeding support, baby care—even toileting assistance for Mom—relieve the new parents' responsibility for doing many of these things. Then upon leaving the hospital, the still-recovering mother and concerned father wave good-bye to their discharge nurse, and drive off with their brand-new baby strapped securely in a car seat.

What happens next? Let's take a peek. . . .

As they arrive home, the new mom and dad are immediately drawn into an unfamiliar world of diapers, nighttime feedings, and tender emotions. For months, they have been planning for this moment—the family settling in at home together for the first time. Tucking the sleeping baby in his bed, they quietly leave the nursery after turning on the electronic room monitor, ready to spend a few brief moments alone.

Five minutes later, reality hits as cries are heard across the hallway.

Is the baby hungry already? Mom tries

> *Our duty is not to gaze at what lies dimly in the distance, but to do what clearly lies ahead.*
> Thomas Carlyle

45

STRESS FACTORS OF THE LEARNING PERIOD

- Hospitalization
- Fatigue—lack of satisfying sleep
- Anxiety about baby's care and health
- Greater financial needs
- Increased family expectations and obligations
- Shift in work distribution within the home: extra laundry, baby care, more at-home meals
- Role transformation: new social status, responsibility, and demands
- Mother's physical changes: healing after birth, establishment of lactation, hormonal variations, body image concerns
- Disruption of usual sexual activity patterns
- Social isolation: more time spent at home, less time available for friends and peers
- Adjustment of siblings (if present) to new baby
- Psychological demands: coping with added responsibilities and expectations; marital changes/conflict; worry about the future; loss of control, especially if baby cries often
- Lack of social support: few available "teachers" to learn new skills from

hurriedly to use the bathroom while Dad attempts to comfort the baby.

He succeeds. After laying the baby down once again, they wonder how long the quiet will last. They decide to eat something. Quick. There's a refrigerated casserole someone sent over; Dad warms it in the microwave as Mom shakily puts dishes on the table.

Suddenly, the phone rings. It's Aunt Louise, calling from Virginia. She wants to hear all about the new baby. Mom takes the call, disguising her muffled chewing and talking between bites. Just before hanging up, she hears the baby crying again. Dad goes to get him.

Mom carries her plate to the living room. Maybe she can hold the baby in the rocking chair and eat at the same time. It doesn't work: she's worried about dropping him and asks her husband to hold him while she finishes her meal.

The baby's crying becomes louder and more insistent. Dad suggests to his wife that she try feeding the baby.

As the baby latches on, Mom's cramps become stronger—a sign that the nursing is helping her body to recover from the birth. The closeness of her newborn son and his sweet sounds of contentment bring her a feeling of calm satisfaction.

- Disrupted daily routines: leave of absence from work and possible discontinuation of outside employment

Dad eats his dinner, then asks Mom if there is anything she could use from the store. "Be back in half an hour, honey," he says.

As the car pulls out of the driveway, Mom looks down at the soundly sleeping baby, takes a deep breath, and sighs. . . .

Understanding Your Children's Stress Sources

"The birth of a child is one of the more stressful events in a person's life," says author Tracy Hotchner in her book *Pregnancy & Childbirth: The Complete Guide for a New Life.* Citing a study that showed that a death in the family is the most stressful life event, she points out that childbirth ranks as the second most stressful. Regardless of how much the parents may have wanted the baby, whether they feel ready for it, or how positive their birth experience may have been, it is still an enormous upheaval in their life.[1]

Although having a baby has always been equated with a family's need for change and adjustment to new responsibilities, life stresses have changed since we were born.

"Parents today are faced with the greatest tasks that have ever been asked of any generation," parent educator Dr. Donna Ewy reminds us. "They are asked to be solely responsible for developing the coming generation without the help of extended families, without the help of concerned neighbors, and without the help of the community. They are being bombarded with 'how-to' advice from the experts, and they are being judged by teachers, doctors, and psychologists on how they are performing. On top of that, mothers are being asked not only to mother but to be an equal part of the earning power of the modern family."

Dr. Ewy asks: "Is it any wonder that parents are overwhelmed with the tasks of parenting? [2]

Understanding new parents' unique stresses and strains allows grandparents to gain valuable insight into how we may offer support at critical moments. The sidebar on pages 46 and 47 summarizes the multiple stress factors confronting childbearing couples today.

A Change in Perceptions

In 1970, a poll of nearly 1,000 women revealed 52 percent of the respondents believed that motherhood was the most enjoyable aspect of being a woman. In second place, at 22 percent, was being a wife. Personal rights and freedom came in third, at 14 percent, and in last place, careers, at 9 percent.

A nearly identical poll conducted in 1983—just thirteen years later—points to the tremendous social upheaval produced by the women's movement during the previous decade. Rights and freedom jumped in popularity, from 14 to 32 percent, assuming the "most enjoyable," top-place position. Career and motherhood tied for second place: 26 percent of the respondents said their careers brought them the most satisfaction, nearly three times the 1970 figure. The number voting for motherhood was divided exactly in half. Perhaps even more significantly, the least important aspect of being a woman to the later poll's recipients was being a wife, which came in a distant last. Down from second place (22 percent) in 1970, the figure in 1983 was 6 percent, a reduction of nearly three-quarters.[3]

These shifts represent one of the most revolutionary changes in women's beliefs about marriage and family life in history. Our daughters' ideas about motherhood may or may not match prevailing trends. Either way, they face increased social pressure in their mothering role as a result of recent cultural changes.

"New motherhood can create a conflict nowadays," Tracy Hotchner explains. "Our society makes it difficult for women to pursue their own goals while providing good care for their children at the same time. Every woman's life (in fact every man's life) has been changed in some way by the ambitious and projected images fostered by the women's movement. A woman may want to get out and work or do something more than housewifing—but there are still the dishes to do, the baby to feed, and no easy solutions to incorporate both."[4]

And it isn't just the women who are feeling the strain. Our sons' expectations have changed, too. Job security in today's competitive workplace demands high-level performance. For men and women who become parents, this job-market mentality may get transferred to the home front, creating confusion and frustration about their new parenting role. As they soon discover, the art of child-rearing is a learn-as-you-go process, without guarantees of "success."

"All parents worry about making mistakes. Not only are mistakes unavoidable, however, but parents learn their job through mistakes," emphasizes renowned pediatrician Dr. T. Berry Brazelton in *Families: Crisis and Caring.* "One reason it can be difficult for successful working parents to adapt to child rearing is that the culture of the workplace is often one of perfectionism and of dependable rewards. In raising a family, on the other hand, rewards are rarely dependable, although they are all the more joyous because of their unpredictability." With unequivocal conviction, he adds, "Perfectionism and the systematic pursuit of success have no place in parenting."[5]

We also know that having children brings unique joys to a family as well. "If becoming a parent were an endless conflict about money, chores, work, the relationship, and social activity, babies would be a lot rarer than they are," Dr. Jay Belsky, professor of Human Development and Family Studies at Pennsylvania State University, observes. "Along with the tumult, the exhaustion, the loneliness, and hurt feelings there are also moments of sublime happiness, moments when the new parent literally begins dancing with joy."[6]

As grandparents, we have a special role to play in fostering this climate of appreciation and celebration. Our genuine enthusiasm about the new baby reinforces the parents' own sense of purpose and meaning—especially when our excitement also takes into account the new parents' needs. While the baby is, understandably, a new source of pride and

> *Once a child is born, it is no longer in your power not to love it or care about it.*
> Epictetus

joy, the grandchild is loved best if we facilitate the parents' rest and comfort during their early transition period to motherhood and fatherhood.

Recognizing New Parents' Concerns

When your children express uncertainty or anxiety about parenting their baby, how will you respond? Because they probably don't expect (or want) you to provide your opinion on whatever subject they may be ventilating about, be prepared to offer thoughtful listening and reassuring affirmation as your children entrust you with their deepest fears and concerns. Keep the focus on your confidence in their competency. Here's a preview of what kinds of statements to expect:

Failure. "Was I really cut out for this?" "Did I make another mistake?" "How did you ever manage to take care of all of us?"

Coping ability. "I feel terrible when the baby cries and won't stop, no matter what I do. Can I cope much longer?" "Being a parent isn't what I thought it would be. How will I deal with this sense of helplessness?" "I didn't expect to experience guilt this soon. Did you feel as overwhelmed by all the time and work involved in caring for a baby as I do?"

Incompetence. "What if I'm not cut out for this?" "What if I fall asleep and can't hear the baby crying?" "What if the baby gets seriously sick and I don't recognize the symptoms?"

Marital harmony. "Why can't Ted see that the baby's needs must be met before we can spend time alone together?" "When will Jane have enough energy to enjoy spending time alone again?"

Baby care. "Is the baby getting enough milk?" "What if anything bad happens to the baby?" "How do I know when to call the doctor?" "Why did the baby get this diaper rash?" "When I'm giving the baby a bath, will I be able to hold and wash him without his slipping out of my hands?" "Is the baby gaining enough (or too little, or too much) weight?"

Responding with Your Support

Hovering grandparents. Meddling grandparents. Unwelcome grandparents. We've all known a few. But how does one avoid being such a grandparent?

The best way to respect your adult children's parenting responsibility is to listen to their preferences, noting the boundaries they are setting for themselves regarding your relationship. Your daughter and son may be eager for you to play a significant part in their family and the life of your grandchild, or they may prefer that you assume a supportive role, as a background player. They may agree with your child-rearing methods and philosophy, or they may choose an entirely different approach.

"The central challenge for grandparents today is to hang in there, no matter what the challenges may be," admits grandmother Eda LeShan in her book, *Grandparenting in a Changing World.* "It calls for great sensitivity on our part to understand ourselves and our children. It calls for an open mind, a belief in common human needs, and feelings, and moral values . . . we are supposed to be more mature than the young couple and should be patient for them to learn through their own life experiences. The main thing is to know we have lived full, varied, different lives before we came together to look through the nursery window."[7]

> ## WHAT NEW PARENTS NEED MOST
>
> Love
> Affection
> Nurturing touch
> Sleep
> Rest and relaxation
> Nutritious food
> Sense of security
> Sense of belonging
> Affirmation of their new identity
> Support from friends and family
> Help with household tasks

Bernardine Heimos, another experienced grandma, agrees. "We need to be patient and not crowd the young parents," she says wisely. "A parent wants to be in the lead with their own child, and they should be. We have to take our cues from them and give them their parenthood, which will certainly not be identical in style with ours, a chance to flower. This is a new family, with its own ways of living, and we do well to keep this in mind and not rush to point out the right way of doing things (*our* way)."[8]

While our children were growing up, we were accustomed to telling them what to do: "Pick up your clothes. "Do your homework." "Don't hit your brother." "Finish college." Even after they become adults, it's our natural inclination to continue guiding their decisions or telling them what we think they should do. And why not? After all, we've been there before.

But it isn't easy when our children decide not to follow in our footsteps. By implication, it seems that one generation is right and the other generation is wrong. Knowing that social realities and expectations have changed relieves some of the pressure: we made the best choices we could in the time when our children born—our children, as adults, are doing the same.

In addition to offering practical help, respecting our children's parenting preferences boils down to this:

Honor their beliefs, thoughts, and feelings. Pay attention to the parents as well as the baby, and encourage them to ask for what they need from you. Ask how you can help.

Maintain your sense of humor. Humor and laughter, when expressed appropriately, is perhaps a grandparent's greatest pressure valve, allowing for the release of frustration and anxiety when tension rises.

Don't compare—or compete. Avoid making comparisons between their experiences and your own: "You slept through the night and were started on cereal at two months." Or "Jenny's baby was potty trained by twenty months." And be supportive of the role their friends and other relatives play in their lives by expressing your appreciation for the gifts and services that people offer. ("What a great idea!" "How kind she was to do that for you." "That was really a thoughtful present, wasn't it?")

> *Serve wholeheartedly . . .*
> Ephesians 6:7

Stick to your own style. If they expect you to fit their expectations of what a grandmother or grandfather should be, talk about what your goals for grandparenting are. Continue to be yourself as everyone adapts to their new roles.

Respect their rules. Discover their preferences and resist any inclination you may have to undermine, improve upon, or otherwise sabotage their parenting choices, including everything from dietary do's and don'ts (no sugar, french fries, ice cream, soft drinks, etc.), to whether or not television is acceptable, to their current religious beliefs. (This may be harder to do than you think.)

Be gracious. Trust that all the things that you learned as a parent are being passed on to your children by example. Reassure your children without expecting them to copy you. Consider yourself a noncritical teacher, available to offer support as needed. When you see a problem, don't assume silence is best: help in your children's crises and share in their joys.

5
Mothering the Mother

What do new mothers need most, besides time, sleep, and money?

They need *mothercare*—the intuitive, unspoken taking care of that nurturing women do best: fixing a favorite meal, neatly folding the laundry, fluffing the pillows, giving a gentle back rub. It is not the baby that needs to be taken care of by the grandmother. It is the new mother.

"Mothering the mother gives the new parent time to cuddle, care for, and love her own infant," explains Dr. Dana Raphael. "It gives her the chance to watch the baby and build a schedule around that infant which is compatible with her own preferences. It allows the mother to enjoy her matrescence [transition to motherhood] and not find it a burden or a nightmare. Help from others allows this to happen."[1]

Across the centuries, mothering the new mother was the grandmother's privileged, expected role. Though times have changed, our daughters' need for mothering after giving birth and during early breastfeeding has not.

"At no time in history have new mothers been expected to do so much for so many with so little help," Dr. William and Martha Sears point out. "Cultures around

Let us not become weary in doing good, for at the proper time we will reap a harvest if we do not give up.
Galatians 6:9

55

the world have always recognized the importance of mothers and babies nesting-in."[2]

The weeks following a baby's birth create a clear need for family support. While it is not always possible for the grandmother to be with her daughter, daughter-in-law, or stepdaughter during the postpartum period, loving support—from wherever it is given—makes a valuable contribution to the new family. And, if we can be there with them, it is even better.

What "Doulas" Do—and Don't Do

Assisting a new mother at this vital time means letting go of being the boss and becoming a servant. It means knowing how to quietly get things done that need doing in a cheerful, supportive manner. It also means recognizing that the new mother will learn from her mistakes as she gets to know her baby and providing a safe place for her to talk about surprising discoveries.

In recent years, a word has been assigned to the person who assumes the mothering-the-mother role: *doula*—the Greek word for "one who serves." The new mother's *doula* may be her mother, mother-in-law, stepmother, sister, friend, her husband, or a professional. It is a "by invitation only" exclusive job to be fulfilled by the person whom the baby's mom thinks will provide her with the best care.

If your daughter doesn't select you, try not to take it personally or be too disappointed. Mother-daughter relationships are complicated family bonds. Know that by supporting her *doula* choice, you will affirm your daughter's decision and enjoy the benefits that come from treating her as an adult. Give other types of support instead. If your own schedule or financial situation prevent you from attending your daughter's homecoming, there are a number of helpful things you can do without being there. (You will find them later in this chapter.)

But let's say that you have been invited to spend time with the new parents, and you will be the one staying with your daughter after your grandchild is born. During this transition time, your daughter may be open to a wider understanding of the indelible link that joins you together, mother to daughter, across two generations and back through time. She may also suddenly encounter a deeper sensitivity for what it means to be the female child of a female.

I have seen this phenomenon happen repeatedly in my practice as a childbirth educator and lactation consultant, and in my own family as well. It is often a time of profound reconciliation as a woman reflects on what it means to be a mother, providing a greater awareness of what her mother went through when she arrived. Birth triggers powerful feelings between a daughter and her mother, often leading to a new (or renewed) closeness, and an appreciation of what motherhood is all about. In the following sections, you'll learn how you can be just the kind of *doula* your daughter needs and deserves.

The Learning Period

The fifth stage of labor begins two hours after a baby is born and lasts six weeks. This is a time of tremendous physiological, anatomical, and emotional adjustment for the mother: Hormone levels shift and sway, the uterus sheds extra cells and shrinks in size, and the breasts swell with milk and other fluids as lactation is established.

The days and weeks immediately following a baby's birth bring many changes to a woman's life. It is not a typical or routine time for her. Instead, it is a period of transition, of moving from one physical state to another, of assuming new roles and responsibilities, and of learning to accommodate necessary changes in one's usual schedules, normal body functions, and everyday habits. Normal life patterns, needless to say, are completely disrupted.

This forty-two day period is a unique and demanding time, when activities are creatively prioritized and rearranged to fit the special needs associated with the postpartum period. "Give her the reward she has earned," says the Hebrew proverb (Proverbs 31:31)—a good word for the new mother, who certainly merits special care and recognition at this time.

As a recuperation vacation after the baby's birth, I consider it mandatory for new moms to refrain from the following activities for at

25 WAYS TO SUPPORT A NEW MOTHER . . .

Here are some suggestions, gleaned from more than 2,000 expectant and new mothers I've taught over the past twenty-two years, of things women say they especially appreciate receiving during the learning period.

- Buy fresh flowers, placed in a lovely vase by her bed or rocking chair.
- Praise her accomplishment.
- Be a good listener.
- Give her a back rub.
- Bring her a new attractive nightgown or leisure outfit.
- Cook a simple, delicious dinner she likes.
- Offer empathy and understanding.
- Protect her privacy while she naps.
- Tell her you will pay for her to receive a facial, manicure, pedicure, or massage.
- Rent a few of her favorite videos.
- Respect her need for quiet.
- Put together a goody basket filled with favorite toiletries.
- Serve her breakfast in bed.
- Focus on the positive.
- Prepare her Sitz bath.
- Compliment the way she holds the baby.
- Buy magazines she likes.
- Fix her favorite snacks.
- Admire her abilities.
- Make her bed up with fresh linens and extra pillows.
- Provide calming comfort.
- Avoid talking about your own childbearing experiences, unless she asks.
- Coordinate brought-in meals.
- Assist with limiting visitors.
- Respect her concerns.

least one to two weeks (no, I'm not kidding!): cooking, cleaning, laundry, grocery shopping, errand running, church attending, and primary care of older children, especially those under five year years old.

The mother's first and foremost responsibility is to rest and relax while she gets to know her new child during their memorable "babymoon." She needs a complete break from her usual activities while her body adjusts to breastfeeding and a post-pregnant state. This is a time in a woman's life when she deserves to be loved, supported, nurtured, pampered, and cared for; in short, to be treated like a queen! A hospital stay of one or two days simply isn't a long enough period for a mother to adjust to her baby and body.

Now comes the problem: Who will perform these tasks for her?

Since new fathers are often exhausted, too, it is an ideal time for one's mother to be involved, assuming the mother-daughter relationship can bear the stress. If you all agree that you, the grandmother, are the right person for the job, here's a one-minute preview of what you can look forward to doing.

The new mother, even if she has borne eight children, benefits from time alone with her baby and short rests at intervals throughout the day and night. Frequent snacks and beverages for her thirst should be served as needed. Since a nursing mother requires about 500 extra calories daily, it helps if her food is appealing as well as nutritious. A pitcher of juice, water, or herbal iced tea should be kept available at all times.

New mothers need mothering. They do not need visitors (who drain their energy), or constructive criticism (which drains their self-esteem), or outdated advice (which drains their patience).

. . . AND WHAT NOT TO DO (ALSO BASED ON MORE THAN 2,000 LIFE STORIES)

- Rearrange her house.
- Say she has never looked better.
- Demonstrate the "right" way to mother.
- Invite your friends over to see the baby.
- Discuss politics (if you disagree).
- Tell her you are exhausted.
- Cook meals she does not like.
- Cancel hired help without asking.
- Say that you wouldn't be there unless you loved her.
- Complain about the pet(s).
- Talk often about your work, health, or marital problems.
- Give gifts she cannot enjoy.
- Make her feel inadequate.
- Start planning where the baby will spend Thanksgiving and Christmas.
- Reorganize the kitchen.
- Buy food she will not eat.
- Offer your advice, unless asked for it.
- Take over the household.
- Compare her with yourself.
- Act like an expert (or a martyr).
- Tell her friends they should be more considerate.
- Comment on her—or anyone else's—size, shape, weight gain, or need for exercise.
- Do too much videotaping or picture-taking.
- Mother the baby.
- Refer to fat grams and calories in foods.
- Disturb her privacy.

Phone calls and visitors can quickly produce fatigue. How does your daughter want to approach them?

When Mom seems like she needs a break, suggest a long shower, warm bath, or a walk outside if the weather is pleasant. Volunteer to watch the baby so she can have some time to herself and be refreshed. She will appreciate having a chance to "get away," uninterrupted by listening for any unusual baby noises. Encourage her to sleep whenever the baby is sleeping. A back rub at least once a day can be relaxing, too.

If you find yourself becoming critical or starting to complain, try not to direct it toward to your son or daughter. Lift your concern to the Lord in prayer or share your feelings with a supportive Christian friend, if needed. Be wise about communicating your concerns and feelings; be gentle and caring about what is said and how the words are spoken.

Remember: this is a brief season in your daughter's life. Soon she will learn to balance her family's needs with her own and return to her busy life. For now, you have a unique ministry opportunity that will be worthy of your best effort.

Planning Your Stay

Before your grandchild arrives, take time to think about what you are and are not willing to do as your daughter's *doula*. Discuss the list with your daughter and son to clarify what each of you expects your role to be after the baby is born.

When will you arrive?

Where will you stay?

How long will you stay?

If you will be staying somewhere else, how many hours per day will you be helping out?

What household tasks are you willing to do, and which will the father do (laundry, meal preparation, grocery shopping, running errands, answering the phone, greeting visitors, caring for pets, cleaning the bathroom, vacuuming, dusting, keeping nursery organized, taking care of older children, watching Baby while Mom sleeps, bottle-feeding Baby, bathing Baby)?

Are there any jobs you are not comfortable doing?

How will you provide for the parents' need for privacy? What activities can you do outside the house every day?

In what ways will you encourage the parents to be independent, resourceful, and creative (vs. dependent, anxious, and inflexible) in their parenting role?

When your daughter or son wants to do something that is totally foreign to you—or that you totally disagree with—how will you thoughtfully share your feelings and preferences?

The "Baby Blues" and Postpartum Depression

> *The best thing to spend on your child is your time.*
> Anonymous

A number of mothers experience mood swings soon after their baby's birth, perhaps as the result of hormone changes, lack of sleep, a reaction to increased responsibilities, or feelings about the birth being an anti-climax. Physical and emotional adjustments to life after pregnancy take time.

The "baby blues," a mild and temporary form of maternal depression, typically occurs within a day or two after birth. While the most common characteristic is crying, the baby blues can also be accompanied by episodes of sleeplessness, irritability, agitation, and exhaustion. As many as four out of every five new mothers encounter these symptoms to some degree, with most feeling a wave of sadness sweeping over them in the first days after childbirth. Usually, these feelings pass quickly, especially if the new mother receives her family's understanding and support. Within a week or two, a sense of equilibrium returns for most moms.

For up to 25 percent of new mothers, these feelings don't subside. Postpartum depression (PPD), a more serious condition that starts later and stays longer than the baby blues, is the reason why.

Postpartum depression typically begins sometime between two

REVIEW OF NORMAL POSTPARTUM CONCERNS AND HELPS

All of the following symptoms are normal and can be eased with the remedies suggested. Naturally, your daughter should report any severe or unusual pain, fever, or discharge, or any other alarming symptom to her physician.

PROBLEM	HELP
Fatigue	Good food; rest—especially when baby rests
Backache	Slow breathing; pelvic rock; massage; heat
Body aches	Warm shower; heating pad
Mood swings	Talk about feelings; accept emotional state as normal
Hot flashes	Fan; light clothing; cool beverages
Menstrual-like cramps (afterpains)	Pain relief techniques; over-the-counter pain relievers
Change in color of vaginal discharge (lochia) back to red	Take it easy; put feet up more often; don't overdo
Sore perineum; itching	Sitz baths; anesthetic spray; Tucks (or 4-inch gauze squares soaked in witch hazel); over-the-counter pain relievers
Gas discomfort after cesarean birth	Pain relief medication; mobility; understand what's causing it; exercises: leg bends, standing and walking, prolonged exhalations with abdominal muscle tightening

Postcesarean incision	Support incision when walking, coughing, laughing, discomfort, etc.; take pain medication as needed; use pillow to cushion incision when holding baby, lying down; call doctor if signs of infection are present
Numbness or bruises in area where the IV was placed	Warm, wet compresses
Abdominal wall flabbiness	Head curls, pelvic rock, patience
Engorgement, leaking breasts, nipple tenderness	Evaluate baby's latch-on position; rotate baby-holding positions; prop towel or cotton pad under breasts as they air dry; try shorter, more frequent feedings; consult a recent breast-feeding manual; contact lactation specialist

weeks to three months after the baby's birth. The exact cause of the condition is still unknown. Hormonal shifts, impaired thyroid function, sleep disturbances, psychological stress, and lack of an adequate support system after the baby's birth are all believed to be contributing factors. Unexpected outcomes and unrealistic expectations associated with parenting may also play a role, including a traumatic birth experience, a less than "perfect" baby, infant crying or sleep problems, and baby-feeding difficulties.

While postpartum depression is an emotionally painful as well as anxiety-producing experience for your daughter, it may encourage you to know that it is a temporary condition, and treatable when diagnosed accurately. If her symptoms include any of the following—excessive sleeping or the inability to sleep, marked change in appetite, intense anxiety or anger, crying for no apparent reason, feelings of helplessness or resentment, self-destructive thoughts, and feelings of inadequacy—

taking the following steps will offer some relief.

Encourage her to talk about how she feels. Suggest that she call a help-line volunteer (or her childbirth educator, midwife, or doctor) to ask for specific information about treatment alternatives, foods to avoid, the amount of sleep needed, recommended reading, ways to reduce stress, what to expect concerning recovery, and if a local support group exists. Depression After Delivery, a postpartum support group with over 80 branches nationwide, is often used for this purpose. Their address is P.O. Box 1282, Morrisville, PA 19067, or, for more immediate assistance, your daughter may call (215) 295-3994. Postpartum Support International, another excellent resource, may be contacted by calling (805) 967-7636, from 8 A.M. to 8 P.M. (Pacific Time).

Give your daughter permission to grieve. All birth represents loss—the loss of being pregnant, the loss of hoped-for realities, and the loss of one's pre-pregnant body, if nothing else. Sometimes the degree of loss is even greater. But even if both your daughter and grandchild are"doing fine," it's important to realize that any amount of loss brings grief. Normal grief is a process which runs its course and eventually leads to emotional restoration; complicated grief that becomes prolonged, intensified, or delayed prevents people from coping with life productively. Because of this, anyone suffering this type of grief benefits from wise counsel and/or appropriate pastoral care. Knowing that it's okay to grieve is an important step in your daughter's healing process.

Assist her in getting more sleep. Interrupted sleep, light sleep, and inadequate amounts of sleep can contribute to depression. As a result, getting enough sleep should be your daughter's number one self-care strategy. If she can learn how to sleep while her baby sleeps—either in her bedroom or in a nursery—she may not need additional help. But if she's worn out from vigilant watchfulness or has other young children to care for, she'll need someone that she can rely on to take over while she shuts the door and snoozes.

Recommend professional help when needed. "Any woman who is undergoing suicidal fantasies or fears she might harm her baby should not waste her time trying to pull herself together but seek good professional help immediately," recommends Carol Dix in *The New Mother Syndrome: Coping with Postpartum Stress and Depression*.[3] A skilled, sensitive counselor will help her take the necessary steps to reduce emotional stress. If, after two weeks, she isn't feeling any better, she should ask to be evaluated for additional treatment with antidepressant medication. Depending on which drug is prescribed, breastfeeding may still be possible if she observes her baby closely for side effects.

In the presence of severe postpartum depression symptoms, *seek medical help now*. If she is experiencing hallucinations, delusions, recurrent morbid thoughts or fears, suicidal fantasies, or fears of harming the baby, it can indicate a rare and serious condition called postpartum psychosis, which occurs in one out of every one thousand women following childbirth. While postpartum psychosis is painful to witness, and you may want to believe it's not happening, waiting and hoping for improvement aren't enough—obtain medical help for your daughter immediately.

Recognize the stresses of early mothering and do what you can to promote your daughter's rest and comfort. Mood swings after childbirth aren't unusual. Small things that might not normally bother your daughter may seem momentarily overwhelming. You can help ease the stress by remembering the five areas where your practical support will be most appreciated:

Sleep: watching Baby while the new mom rests

Meals: food purchasing, coordination, and preparation

General housework: dish washing, laundry, cleaning, etc.

Tension relief: warm baths or showers, massage, relaxation, recreational activities, time outdoors

Emotional support: active listening and loving affirmation

For more information on postpartum support, see Additional Resources, page 204.

Seven Simple Suggestions for Managing Your Time

Once you become involved in your *doula* work, you may find yourself overdoing it. If so, slow down. Take regular breaks. Care for yourself, too.

Make the most of your time, and don't allow temporary stresses and demands to sidetrack you from your primary purpose: providing loving assistance and practical postpartum help to your daughter.

1. Decide what your priorities are.

2. Make a list of what you want to accomplish.

3. Do your least favorite tasks when your energy level is highest.

4. Keep things simple.

5. Hire/find someone else to do work you can't (or don't want) to do.

6. Give yourself a break.

7. Stay in touch with your support network.

Tension is the body's natural response to stress. The trick is, of course, to relax in spite of our tension—not an easy thing when we have too much to do and too little time (or energy) to do it.

Our minds and bodies function together; they're not separate. We know this. But it's an easy thing to forget.

With a new baby, a recovering mother, and a tired father in the house (or in your life), stress build-up is unavoidable. No matter what the source of stress is—physical, emotional, social, spiritual, or something else—make time for relaxation. It will help relieve the pressure.

20 WAYS TO CALM DOWN

- Relax in a warm shower or bath
- Breathe slowly: 6–12 breaths per minute
- Release muscular tension
- Take a quick nap
- Assume a passive attitude
- Set your worry and anxiety aside
- Spend time alone with God
- Slow your pace of activity
- Reflect on your favorite psalm
- Stretch
- Exercise briskly for 30 minutes (walk, swim, etc.)
- Rest for a while outdoors
- Eliminate unnecessary tasks
- Talk to a friend
- Go for a quiet drive
- Read a few chapters of a good book
- Sing, play, or listen to music
- Engage in quiet prayer
- Draw a picture
- Bake bread

To reduce stress quickly:

Find a quiet place. Go where you can spend at least fifteen to twenty away-from-it-all minutes: your room, the garden, the tub, etc.

Dim the lights and turn off the phone. Close the drapes, pull the blinds, close the shutters, turn off bright lights—create a peaceful place where you can rest with minimal distraction.

Get into a comfortable position. A reclining chair or semisitting position, with pillows propped underneath your knees and arms, is best. Play soft music, if you like.

Close your eyes. If you're sleepy or easily distracted with your eyes closed, open them slightly instead.

Let go of your tension. Note any areas of your body where you are carrying tension. Place your hand with gentle care on or near the place where tension is greatest. Rest in God's presence, giving up every heavy burden.

When You Can't Be There

When circumstances prevent you from being present during the learning period, don't despair. There are a number of ways to support your daughter, daughter-in-law, or stepdaughter from a distance when you can't be there.

—Home-delivered meals: some caterers will deliver, serve, and clean up after the meal

—Maid service

—An all-day treat basket: colorfully wrap several presents, marking each with a humorous when-to-open tag: 6 AM (ceramic mug, book of daily devotions, and a box of bran cereal); nap time (eye mask, earplugs, package of new pillowcases); bedtime (bath gel, shower cap, matching sponge, and lip balm); 2 AM feeding (night-light, cassette tape, and personal cassette player, if she doesn't have one)

—Magazine subscriptions (ask for suggestions)

—Gift set of her favorite cologne or perfume

—Relaxing audiotapes or CDs (again, ask first)

—Nursing bras or nightgowns, wrapped with scented lace sachets

—Gift certificate for a certified massage therapist (home visit?)

—Small china clock for her bedside table

—Blank journal and a good pen

—New bed linens

—Engraved crystal rose bowl, posy or bud vase

—Books on tape

—Gift certificate to her favorite store

—Rocking chair or rope hammock (try the J. C. Penney, Spiegel, or L. L. Bean catalogs)

—Porcelain mug with herbal teas, honey, and imported cookies

—Body creams, oils, or soap gel

—Gift certificate to her favorite hair salon (hair care, facial, manicure, or pedicure)

—Stocked pantry (some grocery stores still deliver)

—Current-size clothes to relax in

—Movies-at-home basket: video rental guide, microwave popcorn, "theater" candy, and some favorite videos

—Remembrance album: celebrate her life with a homemade book of favorite photos, accompanied by a family heirloom

—A silver or gold charm that commemorates motherhood (and a charm bracelet, if she doesn't have one yet—this is a wonderful time to start a new tradition)

—New bed pillows (or a new bed!)

—Bouquet of her favorite flowers

—Surprise package by overnight mail (books, tapes, CDs, gift certificate, and cookies work well)

—Professional *doula*: *Doula* services are now available in many communities (see a listing in Additional Resources, page 189. Ask whether one exists near your daughter's home. If she seems interested in obtaining care from a professional *doula*, offer to pay (or help pay) for it. It is one of the best gifts you can give.

6
Supporting Feeding Time:
Breast or Bottle

I knew that we had a dilemma on our hands when Joanna was told that she would not be able to breastfeed her newborn for at least five days. Abigail needed surgery, right away, requiring the rental of an electric pump rental to stimulate and maintain Joanna's milk supply until her baby could nurse.

Was the effort worth it?

Looking at me with exasperated exhaustion, Joanna said, "Mom, I really don't want to do this."

There I stood, a veteran lactation specialist, someone who nursed her children and helped countless women do the same, and my firstborn daughter was considering not breastfeeding. I understood why. After Joanna held her daughter for only a few minutes following birth, Abigail was whisked away to the neonatal intensive care unit, then transferred six hours later to a regional children's hospital twenty minutes away.

Joanna had not even nursed Abigail yet. How could she be expected to know that pumping her breasts would help her to feel a protective closeness to her baby? She was still in shock, the early stages of grief. Should I accept her statement

> *How delicate the skin,*
> *how sweet the breath of*
> *children!*
> Euripides, *Medea*

69

> *Say only what is good and helpful to those you are talking to, and what will give them a blessing.*
> Ephesians 4:29 TLB

as fact—or gently press through the anguish toward Joanna's genuine preference?

Taking a deep breath, I entered a new role as my granddaughter's advocate and my daughter's mothering guide.

"Joanna, I know that using an electric pump is the last thing you feel like doing now. And I'll support your decision, either way. You're right—it *is* a hassle. No question about it. But this is something that only you can do for Abigail. The milk you'll provide is a gift that no one else can give. Why don't you get the pump and just try it? You can always quit later if you decide to."

I saw my daughter's face relax. The pressure was gone. It was her decision. She had someone to unconditionally love and support her if she initiated lactation in her daughter's absence.

An hour later, Joanna used the pump for the first time.

With each passing day, my daughter's determination grew stronger. The pump became her connection with Abigail. After carefully collecting the breast milk, we stored the valuable substance in plastic nurser bags and hand-carried it to the Children's Hospital, up to the third-floor neonatal care unit, where the nurses approvingly added the fluid to Abigail's feedings.

I will never forget the moment when my daughter, surrounded by countless tubes, monitors, buzzers, and blipping lights, breastfed my granddaughter for the first time. I was so proud of them! Abigail took to nursing like a seasoned pro, snuggling close to her mother with the sweet sounds of contented satisfaction. My daughter's tender gift did make a difference—a place of calm in the center of the storm.

Whether or not your daughter or daughter-in-law decides to breastfeed—and for how long—will depend on many factors, including her personal beliefs, family background, social network, health condition, lifestyle, current workplace, and future plans. It will also be influenced by your understanding and support.

Whatever feeding method she chooses, you can make a positive contribution during the postpartum learning period by providing practical help (discussed in the previous chapter) and becoming better acquainted with today's feeding practices.

Breastfeeding Basics

If your daughter or daughter-in-law elects breastfeeding as her infant-feeding method, your role in promoting the process will be especially important. "Without question, a mother will succeed if she is well-equipped with a solid background of information," says Dr. Dana Raphael, "and if she is cherished, pampered, coddled and respected by other adults who sincerely want her to achieve this very personal and tender gift."[1]

Grandparents who offer this kind of respect and support are a welcome addition to the home recovery team. Regardless of your own infant-feeding history, you can play an important role with your calm words and reassuring actions. First it may be helpful to discount the many myths surrounding this most natural of human behaviors.

Myth: Breastfeeding is hard on the mother. Fact: Women who breastfeed their babies gain a number of unique benefits from nursing. Because feedings require taking time out to nurse, moms rest more often; nursing promotes uterine recovery, lessening postbirth bleeding; as moms nurse, prolactin induces relaxation; feedings do not require formula/bottle purchasing, preparation, and cleanup—an added benefit during 3 A.M. feedings.

Myth: Breastfeeding is painful. Fact: During the first few days of breastfeeding, the nipples may be tender; as the milk comes in, the breasts become full. Both are normal—and not painful when treated correctly. Painful breastfeeding indicates something is wrong. Perhaps the baby is not latched on properly, or Mom's breasts are engorged from not nursing often enough. Assistance from a lactation specialist will help solve the problem and quickly ease discomfort.

Myth: Breastfeeding women often cannot produce enough milk to meet infants' nutritional needs. Fact: Breastfeeding is a beautiful process. As baby nurses, hormonal secretions trigger milk production and condition the breasts to produce exactly the right amount of milk. This supply-and-demand process is based on a baby's individual needs by depending on the baby's sucking to stimulate milk production.

Myth: Breastfeeding is a bigger nuisance than bottle-feeding. Fact: With baby's food supply produced at just the right temperature—where it cannot go bad, is instantly available, is perfectly balanced, and comes in the proper amount—breastfeeding is less, not more, of a bother.

Myth: Breastfeeding keeps women confined at home. Fact: Outdated attitudes, not the breastfeeding process, are to blame for making some people feel that nursing belongs in the nursery. But all one needs for discreet, portable breastfeeding are a baby blanket and a two-piece outfit.

Myth: Breastfeeding requires a severely restricted diet. Fact: Most nursing moms, by maintaining a balanced diet and drinking plenty of caffeine-free liquids, find they can eat most types of foods in moderation.

Myth: Breastfeeding will not work if your mother could not nurse. Fact: Genetics and inherited physical traits have not been proven to affect a woman's nursing ability.

Myth: Breastfeeding and working don't mix. Fact: With knowledge and determination, working and nursing can be combined successfully. Women find that expressing and storing breast milk gives them "baby breaks" that focus their thoughts on mothering, producing a comforting closeness during times apart and providing something special that only they can give their babies.

Negative Comments Worth Avoiding

"Maybe the baby isn't getting enough." If your grandchild is soaking six to eight diapers daily, has regular bowel movements, looks healthy (bright eyes, an alert manner, good skin tone), and gains an average of four to six ounces per week during the first month, he is getting enough.

"Your milk looks too watery." Breast milk doesn't look the same as

formula. It has a bluish color closely resembling skim milk, though the fat content varies during the feeding. As the perfect infant food, breast milk provides all the nutrients a baby needs.

"Are you sure you have enough milk?" Breast milk production is based on supply and demand in nearly all cases—each time the baby nurses, the mother's breasts make more milk. Frequent nursings (eight to twelve or more feedings every twenty-four hours) are completely normal—and recommended. Forget the clock. The concept of feeding schedules are unscientific when it comes to physiologically sound breastfeeding.

"I tried to nurse, but it didn't work for me." Think about it: if breastfeeding was designed with an inherently high failure rate, the human race would be close to extinction. Strict feeding schedules, water-and-formula supplements, limited mother-baby contact, and lack of adequate intergenerational support wreak havoc with breastfeeding. Chances are good that you encountered one

KNOWING THE BENEFITS OF BREASTFEEDING

For Baby:
- Provides baby with "living" fluid containing antibodies and organisms, promoting health
- Aids brain development by supplying taurine, a powerful protein
- Produces a dynamic custom-made defense system against infection
- Avoids allergies: no recorded cases of an infant's inability to tolerate mother's milk
- Makes vitamins and minerals more available to the body through better absorption
- Maintains healthy intestinal bacteria growth, eliminating diarrhea
- Eliminates formula purchase, preparation, and storage
- Encourages physical closeness and skin-to-skin contact between mother and baby
- Promotes better oro-facial development in baby due to stronger sucking

For Mother:
- Often delays mother's periods six to twelve months
- Creates exclusive bond between mother and child
- Aids mother's physical recovery after birth
- Adds convenience: breast milk always immediately available at the right temperature, without risk of germs

or more of these challenges before you gave up breastfeeding. Almost any woman who wants to nurse can, no matter how complicated her situation may be, as long as she wants to, and she receives appropriate assistance.

"Just one bottle won't do any harm." In the early weeks of breastfeeding, the baby is learning how to nurse. Because the breast requires a different type of sucking to produce milk than a bottle does, switching between the two can confuse a baby—some babies develop "nipple confusion" and will no longer latch on when offered the breast. The safest thing is to avoid supplemental bottles during the learning period, until breastfeeding is solidly established.

"Solid foods will help him sleep through the night." Baby's digestive systems thrive on human milk. Starting solids sooner than around the middle of the baby's first year increases the likelihood of allergy sensitization and replaces a superior food with an inferior nutrient source. Also, using food as a soothing "filler," instead of fuel in response to natural hunger, predisposes people to obesity. Given these facts, it makes good sense to encourage nighttime sleeping by another method.

"Why do I need to know about breastfeeding? Bottles are just as good." By becoming acquainted with breastfeeding basics, you'll learn about the uniqueness of human milk, gain a greater appreciation for God's grand design for infant nutrition, and acquire knowledge to enable you to offer substantial lactation support. Expert status is not required.

Bottle-feeding Basics

While no commercial preparation is a completely satisfactory, risk-free replacement for mother's milk, current formula products are a widely chosen alternative for infants. The following guidelines will bring you up-to-date on today's bottle-feeding recommendations.

Do use the variety, color, type of nipple, and brand of bottle, whether disposable or refillable, that your daughter selects. If you purchase bottles to keep at your house, be sure to sterilize them before their first use: wash on dishwasher's bottom rack in a protective "cage" or immerse in boiling water for one minute, remove with tongs, then let cool. Do not stock up on nipples or pacifiers until you know what kind your grandchild will accept; babies can be choosy. Also, use only the brand of formula recommended by your grandchild's doctor and do not offer regular cow's milk until after baby's first birthday.

Do be careful not to contaminate formula. Unlike in the past, today's ready-to-feed infant formulas are presterilized. Unopened formula may be stored until the package expiration date arrives, but once opened, formula can "go bad" when handled improperly. Refrigerate opened premixed formula or concentrated liquid formula; if the remainder isn't used within forty-eight hours, toss it out—do not freeze it. Any formula left in the bottle after feeding should be thrown away because it has been mixed with bacteria and saliva in Baby's mouth. Never use leftover formula that has been left unrefrigerated for more than three hours.

Do not bother with boiling Baby's bottles. Use disposable nurser bags to hold formula in a plastic bottle—a convenient way to avoid bacteria and minimize air swallowing. If reusable bottles are Mother's choice, use a dishwasher to sterilize bottles and feeding equipment. Reassemble bottles before storing, then store in covered container.

Do become familiar with available infant formulas. Most full-term babies use a milk-based formula made from non-fat milk and a milk protein called demineralized whey. Vegetable oils are used to replace the butterfat naturally found in cow's milk to provide essential nutrients. Babies who experience difficulties with this type of formula are often switched to a soy-based formula. In some cases, a protein hydrolysate formula may be recommended if the baby is unable to digest or tolerate other formulas.

Do watch the flow of formula as Baby sucks. Air bubbles rising in a steady stream up the side of the bottle, with Baby's mouth moving rhythmically, indicates all is in order. Gulping means the formula is flowing too fast. Is the nipple cracked or too large for your grandchild? If Baby is actively sucking without getting much milk, the flow is too slow. Check the nipple opening: perhaps the nipple is clogged, the screw cap is too tight, or the nipple opening is not large enough. To test the size, invert the bottle and shake it—the liquid should leak out at two to three drops per second and, if necessary, enlarge the nipple opening with a heated needle. If Baby sucks in a quivering motion, the nipple may be collapsed—removing the nipple from his mouth will break the vacuum.

Do burp baby once or twice during feedings when baby's sucking pauses, and once afterward. All babies swallow some air when they take a bottle. Burping releases the air, alleviating gas buildup and stomach discomfort. Keeping a burp cloth handy, use whatever position seems most comfortable—and effective—for burping baby: put him against your chest or over your shoulder, gently rubbing and patting his back as you rock; place him in a sitting position (bent slightly forward) on your lap, supporting his head and chest with one hand as you pat his back with the other hand; lay him on your lap, stomach down, supporting him with your hand and rubbing his back.

Do carefully heat bottles in the microwave. According to recent research published in the journal *Pediatrics*, you can safely warm formula in the microwave by following these instructions: 1. Heat at least four ounces at a time; 2. Stand the bottle in the oven; 3. Heat four-ounce bottles on full power for no longer than thirty seconds, and eight-ounce bottles for no longer than forty-five second; 4. Replace the nipple, then invert the bottle ten times (do not shake it). Most babies prefer their formula slightly warm, though the formula should feel cool to your touch. Shake a few drops onto the back of your hand or onto your tongue to test the temperature.

Do hold your grandchild whenever she needs to be fed. Minimize air swallowing by tilting the bottle. This causes milk to fill the nipple and air bubbles to rise to the bottom of the bottle. Allowing for normal variations in appetite, feed Baby until he seems satisfied. Avoid arm fatigue by switching sides at each feeding. Bottle propping encourages dental decay, especially if Baby falls asleep nursing on his bottle. The snuggling time associated with feedings will help bonding for both of you.

Promoting a Comfortable Feeding Environment

If you are helping to care for the new mother, you can do many things to make feeding time relaxing and successful. Dim lights, soft music (or just peace and quiet), pillows, and a comfortable rocking chair help Mom to tune out the world and enjoy being alone with her baby.

Discourage interruptions. Your presence will be especially welcome when the doorbell or telephone rings. When possible, turn the telephone ringer off. Unless there is an emergency, callers can wait. When you are not available to answer the door, hang a notepad with a pen out front next to a message of your choice.

Provide a pitcher of chilled water, milk, or juice. Or fix a warm beverage tray with herbal tea (one teaspoon of fenugreek tea steeped in boiling water for about five minutes boosts the milk supply, or use a commercial brand of "Mother's Milk" tea), hot cider, or Postum in an attractive mug, with a favorite magazine placed beside it. Serve her a healthful snack, such as a fruit salad, whole-grain sandwich, toasted bagel with Neufchatel cheese, or blueberry bran muffin (see recipes in Additional Resources, page 196.

Especially for Nursing Moms

Assist Mom with a shower or soak in the tub before nursing (a Sitz bath during postpartum: four inches of water, with the upper part of the body wrapped in a warm towel or blanket, for ten to twenty minutes; add more hot water as needed) Warm water encourages milk flow and eases tension.

Support Mother's posture. Pillows are used as necessary, whether Mom is sitting up in bed or in a rocking chair. By placing pillows under the baby's body and beneath the arm cradling the baby's head, Mom's back, shoulder, and neck muscles have a greater chance of

> *Purposeful giving is not . . . apt to deplete one's resources; it belongs to that natural order of giving that seems to renew itself even in the act of depletion. The more one gives, the more one has to give—like milk from the breast.*
> Anne Morrow Lindbergh,
> *Gift from the Sea*

relaxing. If Mom is sitting up, a stool or large pillow may be used to raise her knees to a more comfortable level; if she is lying down, a few pillows tucked in behind her will promote back and abdominal muscle relaxation.

Adjust the baby's position. When nursing, the baby's head should be on an even plane with his body; it should neither bend forward nor arch backward. Turning the baby so that the nursing couple are "tummy to tummy," rather than holding the baby's body so that it is facing upward or outward, ensures a better latch-on. If the baby insists on thrusting his arm out, the baby may be wrapped securely, in swaddling fashion, with his arms tucked inside a blanket, or his hand can be tucked under Mom's arm.

What About Pacifiers and Thumb-sucking?

By the time your grandchild was born, he was an expert at sucking. After months of thumb-sucking in the womb (one of his earliest neuromotor activities), he arrived with an intense need to continue the practice. He'll abandon this pursuit eventually, but for now at least, sucking promotes his physical survival and emotional well-being.

Some babies have a more intense sucking need than others. Providing for this need by allowing thumb-sucking, offering the baby a pacifier, and frequent breastfeeding, makes sense. Through a trial-and-error process, your daughter or daughter-in-law will decide which ways work best for her and the baby.

Not all grandparents are accustomed to parents letting their children suck their thumbs or use a pacifier, and few grandmothers today considered their breast to be the primary pacifier when their babies were born. Do not be surprised if you start to feel unsure about any of these practices as a result—your own background naturally affects your comfort level.

Here are the reasons that these practices are common today:

—Recent studies show that babies thrive when their sucking needs are met.

—Sucking soothes babies.

—Sucking is not only designed for obtaining food: infants suck differently when taking milk and when soothing themselves.

—If used in addition to—but not as a replacement for—human nurturing, pacifiers and thumb-sucking are highly recommended for promoting peace and quiet during car rides, doctor's exams, sermons, and other key moments.

Becoming the Grandparent
Your Kids Want You to Be

7
Sharing Your Concerns

When a grandchild is born, an opportunity for greater family involvement arrives, no matter what our life circumstances. It is a time for reassessing our priorities and discovering what part we will play in our grandchildren's lives.

Until just a generation ago, grandparents tended to live nearby—within an hour's driving distance, or less—and remain closely involved with their children's families. Most grandmothers stayed at home, even after raising their children. Now, long-distance separations between grandparents and grandchildren are common, and more grandmothers are college graduates—many with full-time professional careers. Millions of today's grandparents travel extensively every year, eat many of their meals in restaurants, participate in weekly recovery group meetings, and exercise regularly. A sizable number are divorced or remarried; of these, a significant percentage are also committed stepparents.

Unlike our grandparents, we are more likely to be working outside the home. We lead active, busy lives that center on our marriages, vocations, and personal interests (church, community service, continuing education, and so on) instead of on our adult children. On the whole, we have higher incomes, greater mobility, and a wider variety of lifestyle options than our grandparents had. Ranging in age from our late thirties to our seventies and beyond, we are just as likely to be running in a regional marathon, leading a Bible study, or arguing a legal case as we are to be knitting baby booties.

The question is, how will we choose to approach our new privileges and responsibilities?

Learning how to be a grandparent, like learning to be a parent, does not happen overnight. Given our packed-full schedules and the life transitions associated with growing older, our grandparenting role will not stay exactly the same across the seasons—it will develop and change over time.

The rules that govern this new adult relationship may be unspoken or clearly spelled out. How will we communicate what we will and will not do? What do our children expect of us as grandparents? What are our expectations of them? Of our grandchildren?

Through it all, we can recognize the unique bond we share with our grandchildren by reminding ourselves of our important position within our families. We can enjoy our grandchildren without carrying the responsibility for rearing them. With our own children grown at last, we join them as part of the supporting cast on a new family's stage.

Setting Limits

As grandparents, we cannot protect our grandchildren from life's myriad of trials and troubles. As families, we cannot completely avoid controversy, either.

It helps to talk about the values, rules, beliefs, and expectations our children will use while raising our grandchildren and what part they want us to play in backing up their parenting role. We will not always agree with their point of view. If in the heat of the moment we are suddenly assigned a role that we are not prepared for (or are unwilling to assume), it is a guaranteed formula for producing family friction. On the other hand, our grandchildren—and children—can benefit from our well-earned wisdom, calm reasoning, and durable experience.

Because our children need ongoing parenting and grandparenting support, we must learn what their expectations are concerning our role and talk openly with them about how we want to be involved in their lives. The best way to do this is by communicating our ideas, preferences, advice, and suggestions "up front," before troublesome topics create painful conflict.

To help set the boundaries that will define mutually acceptable behaviors, discuss the following topics to create clear expectations (but not all at once!).

Visits. How often, and how long, do your children prefer that you visit?

Advice. Have they asked for it?

Gifts. Do your children have a preference about the number, cost, and type of gifts?

Financial and emotional support. Are you offering either (or both) because they need it or because you need to?

Baby-sitting. How much are you willing to offer?

Parenting issues. If you disagree with your children's parenting practices and they expect you to take a similar approach when caring for your grandchild, what will you do or say?

In-laws. How will you avoid, or minimize, competition for your grandchild's love and affection?

Child behavior guidelines. When your grandchild visits, what will your "house rules" be? How do your rules differ from your children's?

Meals, snacks, and desserts. Are there any foods that your children don't want you to feed to your grandchild?

Religious practices. Do your beliefs differ from your children's? If so, are there any topics or activities related to your faith that they prefer you not to share?

Improving Communication Skills

While clear communication with

> *Most grandparents . . . try hard not to interfere. On the other hand, they have had experience, they feel they've developed judgment, they love their grandchildren dearly, and they can't help having opinions.*
> Dr. Benjamin Spock

our children can help prevent unnecessary conflict, disagreements between adults are normal. Coping with varying viewpoints, however, requires more than a little patient understanding. As parents, our children are bound to approach more than a few things differently than we did. A new mother may welcome her baby into the family bed for breastfeeding and cuddling while the grandmother believes the practice is harmful. The young parents may plan a backpacking trip to Europe, while the grandparents can't imagine taking a four-month-old infant on a transatlantic journey. When the expectant father tells his dad that he plans to tie the baby's umbilical cord himself, Grandpa may shudder (or pass out!).

Instead of trying to eliminate our existing differences, we can accept the inherent friction of family life

THE 25 MOST COMMON AREAS OF INTERGENERATIONAL DISAGREEMENT

- Outlook on parenting and childrearing: values, goals, and expectations
- Child discipline
- Money
- Grandparent's role: level of involvement in children's family
- Personal beliefs: religion, politics, etc.
- Lifestyle differences
- Divorce, remarriage, step-parenting, and child custody (grandparents' visitation rights)
- Grandparent baby-sitting: how much, where, and when
- Vacations: pressure to visit during work or school breaks when families live far apart
- Where to spend the holidays
- Career and day care plans
- Living location
- Length of visits
- "Spoiling": how much to hold the baby
- Pacifiers
- Breast-feeding vs. bottle-feeding; scheduled vs. demand feeding
- Bedtime and sleeping location: flexible or strictly scheduled; early or late; family bed or crib
- Weaning
- Potty-training
- Clothing choices
- Gifts
- Entertainment: TV, movies, videos, electronic games, etc.
- Schooling choice: public, private, parochial, or at-home?
- Housekeeping style
- Toys: parents' vs. grandparents' preferences

while teaching our grandchildren a valuable lesson: we respect our children's parenting responsibility for choosing the values, rules, and goals that govern their family, and we expect our children and grandchildren to respect our values, rules, and goals when they are in our home. Recognizing and respecting these differences makes a positive contribution to our grandchildren's lives.

"You are a parent forever, even after you become a grandparent," explains psychiatrist Dr. Arthur Kornhaber in *Grandparent Power!* "That gives you a mandate to share the wisdom and experience that you have accumulated throughout life. So persevere. If you are not blatantly bossy and keep the lines of communication open and show that you're a good listener, and that you're not a preacher but a teacher, you will win the young people's trust and you'll all stand to benefit—including your grandchildren-to-be."[1]

Because he realizes that such communication poses challenges, Dr. Kornhaber says: "I'm not saying this will be easy, but I promise you that you will grow through the process." He

PRIVILEGES OF GRANDPARENTHOOD

- Grandparents may share their beliefs and preferences.
- Grandparents may express their thoughts and feelings.
- Grandparents may say no.
- Grandparents may talk about their role expectations with their children.
- Grandparents may decide how involved and available they plan to be at the present time.
- Grandparents may live their own lives without having to assume their grandchildren's child-rearing responsibilities.

RESPONSIBILITIES OF GRANDPARENTHOOD

- Grandparents are responsible for recognizing their children's parenting goals and expectations.
- Grandparents are responsible for reinforcing parental decisions.
- Grandparents are responsible for learning about and understanding today's trends in childbearing and child care.
- Grandparents are responsible for acknowledging that they serve as family models to their children and grandchildren.
- Grandparents are responsible for discovering how to help by openly discussing their ideas and plans with their grandchildren's parents in advance.
- Grandparents are responsible for loving their grandchildren.

recommends scheduling regular family meetings (over the phone or, preferably, in person) with an actual agenda and running them according to the following guidelines.

Conducting a Family Meeting

Choose the right time and the right place. Meet in a prearranged location in a pleasant, stress-free setting like a quiet restaurant or a park. If the meeting is at your house, serve a snack or coffee and dessert.

Don't issue orders. Adult children are not open to being told what to do. You will be much better off having a two-way conversation.

Avoid falling into an advice-giving pattern in the heat of a disagreement. "When you avoid blaming and bossing, and treat young people with respect," Dr. Kornhaber points out, "you will find that they not only stop resisting your help, but are in fact hungry for it."[2]

Steer clear of sentences that begin with "You." Share your opinions and feelings as "I" statements: "I think what's worrying you most is . . .", "I'll admit it bothers me when . . .", "I understand that you are . . .", "I see your point of view about . . .".

Communicate your feelings and preferences. "Your children may seem to be pushing you away, but never have they needed you more," points out Dr. Kornhaber. "Also, while there may be intergenerational confrontations that belie this, keep in mind, in the deepest sense, your children will always love and need you."[3] How you express yourself helps or hinders your children's ability to listen to what you say, so deliver your message in such a way that it is more likely to be received.

Using Active Listening

As a parent, you are probably well-accustomed to hearing your children share their questions and concerns. Now that they are parents themselves, your listening ability still affects the quality of your relationship. Here are several suggestions[4] on how to empathize effectively:

—Arrange for a time when you're alone (or in a separate room) and it isn't likely that you'll be interrupted.

—Set aside what's currently on your mind. Noises, worries, physical discomfort, and other distractions interfere with your listening ability.

—Think about what it's like to actually be your child, not just what you might feel like in her circumstances.

—Listen and watch for your child to identify her thoughts and emotions: how does she appear to be feeling? What is the sound and rhythm of her speech? Is she tense or relaxed?

—Name the emotions silently, as accurately as you can. The emotions expressed may be subtle or blatant, obvious or hidden. What are you seeing, hearing, and sensing that confirms what the feelings are?

—Reflect on the feelings. After identifying what you think the feeling is, let your child know what

> ## DEFENSIVE LISTENING BEHAVIORS—AVOID 'EM!
>
> - Explaining
> - Asking questions to satisfy your curiosity
> - Criticizing
> - Competing—talking about your own experiences
> - Daydreaming
> - Complaining
> - "Sugarcoating"—denying her feelings by putting an optimistic spin on your responses
> - Advising without being asked for your opinion
> - "Tuning out"—assuming you know what she's going to say before she says it or that you've already heard it before
> - Completing her sentences
> - Judging
> - "Distancing"—acting as if you already know how she feels
> - Allowing yourself to be distracted as an escape from discomforting emotions
> - Feeling frustrated or impatient
> - Interrupting
> - Projecting—thinking of what you might feel in her position

you are picking up. Say something like, "It seems to me you're feeling . . ." or "I hear you saying . . ." or "It sounds like you are . . .".

—Focus your response on the person instead of on the content of what is being said. Recognize and affirm your child for who she is, instead of what you want her to be.

—Curb defensive listening behaviors. If you find yourself doing any of the things listed in the sidebar while you're listening, it will interfere with your ability to actively hear and respond to your child.

Establishing Verbal Boundaries

Picture an action that conveys caring: a courteous gesture, the warmth of a gentle embrace, a cool cloth placed on a feverish brow, the sweetness of a genuine smile, a kind word spoken to provide reassurance, an offer to help.

Compare these to what can happen when wills clash and tempers flare up: words are spoken that pierce the heart, eyes flash with harsh judgment, a hand shoves to push away, stony silence is the response to real need, a back is turned to prove a point—a declaration that "I'm not with you."

> *In case you're worried about what's going to become of the younger generation, it's going to grow up and start worrying about the younger generation.*
> Roger Allen

Our words and actions are simply the external reflections of what is going on inside our minds and heart. We possess the ability to hurt and to heal, to tear down or build up those we claim to love. The ways we choose to express our inner thoughts and feelings matter. Our actions can bring peace, or battles, to the home front.

Criticism within families is a prime source of fuming, feuding, and fighting. We expect criticism from colleagues and casual friends, but we have a much greater emotional investment within our most intimate relationships. Our family members and closest friends are supposed to love and accept us unconditionally. Yet no one can love us perfectly.

How can we constructively communicate our expectations and desires concerning family relationships? If we took as much care in communicating with our adult children as we do with people we respect at church and work, it would significantly reduce family tension.

Understanding our children as they actually are—not who we want them to be—builds mutual trust and respect. Out-of-bounds criticism can quickly destroy both.

Out-of-bounds criticism is always destructive. It is never okay to verbally belittle, bash, or berate someone else. Whether the off-limits criticism is offered in public or in private, it's still harmful to the receiver of the message and to the relationship. If you grew up with a verbally abusive parent, you are well acquainted with the long-lasting effects of toxic words.

Before you criticize, stop and think carefully about what you intend to say and why you want to say it. Ask yourself:

Is this for my child's benefit or mine?
What will he gain from what I'm saying?
Will she accept my criticism?
Is the change I expect from him reasonable?
Can she make the change I expect?

In-bounds criticism, on the other hand, is an acceptable way to communicate your desire for behavior changes. It takes into account both parties' expectations, is given at the appropriate time, and contains a constructive, instead of destructive, message.

If your child will not benefit from your criticism, is not capable of changing, or cannot accept what you have to say, it's time to rethink your position and approach. If you still believe that your viewpoint is valid and valuable, you will need to clearly state what the purpose of your criticism is and what the desired outcome or action will be.

Before you say anything, think ahead. Ask yourself: "What do I want or expect from my daughter or son?" If you know the answer to this question and understand what the desired behavior is, you may prefer to express your opinion in a different way.

Explain your expectations. Take time to clearly explain what you expect. Avoid subtle hints and silent messages. Say what you expect up front, before misunderstandings arise.

Finally, consider asking. It is easy to assume that others know what we are concerned about. Instead of telling your child what you want, try asking first.

QUICK TIPS FOR CONFRONTING CONFLICT

- Once the disagreement comes to light, it needs to be discussed as soon as possible.
- The person with whom the conflict originated may need to be heard first while the other one listens.
- If you are angry or upset, you are likely to find it difficult (if not impossible) to listen with love or sensitivity.
- Take time to reduce your stress level before the discussion; tell your child that you'll listen once you've had a chance to calm down.
- During your conversation, use "I" (vs. "You") messages.
- Let your child know that you accept the way she feels—it doesn't mean you've given in, negated your own feelings, or agree with her point of view.
- You may find that one of these strategies, or a combination of them, will work for you:

  Compromise. You both yield, moving toward common ground.

  Coexistence. You agree to disagree.

  Concession. One of you, though not always the same one, submits t the other.

  Conciliation. You commit your selves to working together to make your views compatible.

Confronting Conflict Constructively

Family conflicts arise no matter how much we respect and value one another. At such times, good communication and sensitive listening go a long way toward creating family harmony and mutual understanding.

"Contrary to popular belief, conflict is not necessarily bad. In fact, conflict can be a powerful tool for strengthening relationships and solving problems," assert Dr. Frank Minirth, Dr. Paul Meier, and Stephen Arterburn in *The Complete Life Encyclopedia.*

"When two people or two groups enter into an experience of conflict, many positive results can emerge—if the people involved in the conflict understand how to manage conflict in a caring and constructive way."[5] To achieve this goal, they recommend using these guidelines.

1. Learn to separate major issues from minor issues.

2. When conflicts arise, confront them as soon as possible.

3. Stick to the subject at hand.

4. In times of conflict, avoid generalizing; be specific.

5. Avoid personal insults and character assassination.

6. Express real feelings; avoid intellectualizing.

7. Demonstrate unconditional love and affirmation, but avoid patronizing.

8. Demonstrate empathy and reflective listening.

9. Affirm publicly, confront privately.

10. Confront to heal, not to win.

"In any conflict, the only real winners are the ones who learn how to manage that conflict to bring about a positive, constructive resolution," concludes the Minirth-Meier team. "When we approach conflict with courage, honesty, and love for the other person, conflict is no longer the enemy of relationships. It becomes our ally."[6]

A Time to Forgive

"Love means never having to say you're sorry," declared the film *Love Story* in the 1970s. But this idealistic phrase doesn't fit who we really are. The relationships we share with other family members test us. Within the framework of the family our self-centeredness gets ground away by the friction of opposing needs, outlooks, desires, and personalities.

Learning to say we're sorry and to extend forgiveness to each other promotes family peace. Each person needs to learn to develop the capacity for seeing beyond his or her own viewpoint in order to understand where another family member is coming from.

The way we cope with disagreements, disappointments, and communication "disasters" directly influences family relationships. When we butt our heads up against one another's walls we get bruised. No matter how hard we try, we can't love perfectly.

What can we do about all those bumps and bruises? We can

—Accept bruised feelings as an inevitable part of family life.

—Acknowledge our imperfections and be gracious about acknowledging them in others.

> *The just man walketh in his integrity: his children are blessed after him.*
> Proverbs 20:7 KJV

—Learn and practice the art of making appropriate apologies—saying we're sorry.

—Ease conflict through improved communication.

—Find ways to express our anger appropriately and fairly.

—Refuse to nurture feelings of self-pity, resentment, emotional dependency, and dissatisfaction.

—Be faithful in forgiving others.

8
Promoting Your Grandchild's Health and Safety

Caring for one's grandchild without his parents around is a very different experience from sharing his attention with our children. We can coo, coax, and coddle to our heart's content. Whether it is only for one hour or an entire weekend, the time spent is well worth the effort. A whole new world opens before us as we encounter life through a child's eyes once again. And this time around, we have greater freedom to revel in the wonder of it all.

By the time your grandchild is born, you may feel quite out of practice with caring for a baby or toddler. Don't worry; your much-used skills are probably not as rusty as you might think. With just a little practice and patience, you will be a pro again in no time.

In this chapter you will find tips to help you face sudden unwelcome surprises—and tips for preventing them from happening. If your grandchild spends time at your house, you will need to childproof accessible areas. A home safety checklist is included to help you in this essential endeavor. There are also suggestions for caring for a sick child and steps to follow when dealing with emergency situations.

Baby-sitting Basics

Before baby-sitting your

> *God is our refuge and strength, an ever-present help in trouble.*
> Psalm 46:1

BABY-SITTER'S REFERENCE SHEET

Parent's location _____(Name and address)

Phone number _____

Expected time of return _____

EMERGENCY PHONES:

EMS _____

POLICE _____

FIRE _____

Physician (name/phone)

_____

Hospital (name/phone)

_____

Neighbor (name/phone)

_____

24-hour pharmacy (name/phone)

_____

Special instructions

_____

_____

_____

_____

grandchild at his house, review the "house rules" with your son or daughter and take notes. Ask about:

Behavior expectations. Eating, play, and sleeping routines—general instructions (when, where, what, with whom, etc.).

Location of foods and supplies. Bottles, snacks, diapers, special baby-care products, etc.

Potty patterns. Diapering and changing; current training status.

Planned activities. Bathing, meals, staying in versus going out.

Emergency information. Home address and necessary numbers;

neighbor's names and phone numbers; fire and/or security alarm location and operation; fire escape routes; location and instructions for use of emergency items (flashlights, fire extinguishers, first-aid kit, circuit breaker or fuse box).

Discipline and developmental matters. Parent's rules; possible trouble areas (tantrums, refusal to go to bed at night, etc.) and what to do about them; supervision requirements ("Carrie tends to bump her head on the coffee table if she tries to stand near the sofa").

Special concerns. Current medications and health needs; fears and how to cope with them; sibling rivalry.

Phone calls, visitors, and deliveries. Are any expected? How should they be handled?

Security items. Door lock instructions (including interior doors); location of keys.

Household equipment use. Appliances, computer, entertainment center, and recreational items (pool, hot tub, boat), if applicable.

Pet care and habits. Letting pet in or out; food and water needs; sleeping location; safety level with children and visitors.

At Your House

When your grandchild comes to your house, there are even more things to think about. While his parents have no doubt turned their home into a completely child-safe environment, your home may no longer qualify as such! Use the checklists in the sidebar as a guideline when evaluating the safety of your home and yard. Concerning the installation of childproof devices, consider first whether your situation requires making a permanent change to promote your grandchild's health and safety.

Infrequent visits from toddlers call for temporary childproofing and restricted entry (using gates to prevent your grandchild from entering the kitchen; locking the doors to rooms that aren't childproof), whereas frequent visits benefit from the use of more extensive protective measures (childproof latches on kitchen cupboards; locked medicine cabinets; bathtub and toilet safety features) to allow your grandchild wider access to your home.

FOOD AND KITCHEN CHECKLIST

- Are hot containers and hot drinks always kept out of reach?
- Have we purchased and installed a stove guard and knob covers?
- Do I turn pot handles away from the front of the stove when I'm cooking?
- Do I boil or fry foods on the back burners whenever possible?
- Are there appliance latches on the refrigerator, dishwasher, microwave, and trash compactor?
- Do I keep the dishwasher door closed and add detergent only when I'm ready to run it?
- Are knives and other potentially hazardous utensils kept out of reach?
- Have cabinet and drawer guard latches been installed?
- Are toxic substances and cleaning compounds kept in cabinets with child-proof locks?
- Do I always avoid carrying my grandchild when I am holding a cup of coffee or other hot liquid?
- Are countertop appliances unplugged after each use?

BED AND BATH CHECKLIST

- Are my cosmetics, perfumes, hair treatments, and other beauty-related products stored safely behind doors with childproof locks?
- Have toxic cleaning products been placed in cabinets with childproof locks, along with any medicines, vitamins, and mineral supplements, medicated creams and ointments, and other poisonous substances?
- Is the toilet lid secured with a safety latch to prevent water play?
- Do I immediately drain the bathtub after I use it?
- Has the child's bathtub been updated for safety (nonskid appliqués, childproof knob covers, soft spout cover, etc.)?
- Is the hot water temperature set at 120° F, hot enough to clean dishes and clothes, yet not be scalding to skin?
- Do I test the water temperature with my wrist or a bath thermometer before I put my grandchild in the tub?
- Do I ever leave my grandchild (under five years old) unattended in the bathtub?

LAWN AND GARDEN CHECKLIST

- Are the garage and yard free of poisonous plants (oleander, holly, azalea, geranium, scotch broom, daffodil bulbs, etc.)?
- Does my yard have any poison oak, poison ivy, or other noxious plant where my grandchild can reach it?

- Am I certain to never leave the child unattended in or near water (hot tub, pool, pond, lake, etc.)?
- Has all hazardous lawn equipment been stored in a safe place? If I own a rotary lawnmower, does it have a protective shield?
- Do I safely store barbecue utensils, lighter fluid, and related cooking items?
- If I own an electric or gas grill, is its energy source securely shut off when I'm not using it?
- Do I closely supervise outdoor play?
- Is outdoor play equipment in good repair and known to be safe?
- Are fence gates kept closed to prevent my grandchild from wandering out of the yard?

GENERAL HOUSEHOLD CHECKLIST

- Do above-ground windows remain closed or always stay protected so that children can't fall?
- Is there any empty refrigerator or freezer in which children might play?
- Have I put all insecticides, animal poisons, fertilizers, cleaning compounds, and paint and gardening products in a locked location?
- Are all toxic substances, including medicines and stain removal products, stored in childproof cabinets?
- Is shoe polish kept out of reach?
- Have I checked the house thoroughly for lead hazards and followed up on potential sources of poisoning (particularly on any old painted furniture or imported ceramic dishes)?
- Have old broken toys been discarded? Do any toys at our house have sharp edges or small parts that can be easily removed or swallowed?

ELECTRICAL HAZARD CHECKLIST

- Do I promptly replace frayed or worn-out electrical cords?
- Are excess electrical cords kept out of reach?
- Are there outlet covers on all outlets not currently in use?
- Do I unplug and put away electrical appliances that I normally operate near the tub or sink when water is in use?
- Are electric bulbs immediately replaced to avoid empty light sockets?

FIRE HAZARD CHECKLIST

- Have smoke detectors been installed and maintained according to current department of public safety guidelines?
- Do I keep currently charged, easily reached fire extinguishers in places

where fires are most likely to happen (in the kitchen, your car, by the outdoor barbecue grill, etc.)?
- Have I developed and practiced a fire exit plan?
- Are all heating devices (fireplace, space heaters, wood-burning stove, etc.) guarded by a protective shield or screen?

FIRST-AID CHECKLIST

- Am I currently trained in CPR and choking aid?
- Do I always keep a bottle of syrup of ipecac on hand in case of accidental poisoning?
- Are emergency phone numbers clearly posted?
- Do I have my grandchild's health insurance information, written on a current medical treatment consent form, in a place where I can quickly find it?
- Have I familiarized myself with an up-to-date first-aid handbook that can be easily located?
- Is there a first-aid kit available in my house and do I know what's effective and what's not? (Iodine, for example, cleans cuts and kills germs, but it's irritating to the skin and highly poisonous; Mercurochrome looks pretty, but is ineffective. Water, antibacterial soap (or Betadine, if you prefer to use a nonstinging iodine preparation), and hydrogen peroxide work wonders with most scrapes, small cuts, and sores.) Which physician will treat my grandchild if the need arises?

If you will be caring for your grandchild alone, prepare yourself for a range of emergencies; If one or both parents are readily available, the responsibility for supplying first-aid or obtaining medical care belongs to them.

Given these and other considerations, think about which child-proofing steps are reasonable for you to take right now, given the amount of time your grandchild will be with you, the areas of your home that you feel comfortable sharing with your grandchild, and your normal level of responsibility. Review, update, and expand your list as your grandchild grows and circumstances change.

The best defense against childhood injury can be summed up in one word: prevention. By childproofing your home, you can significantly decrease the risk of life-threatening injury and accidental death.

Be Prepared

There is nothing quite so comforting as having a grandparent who knows how to provide care after a minor injury occurs—a Band-aid applied to a small cut, soothing ointment gently covering an insect bite, tweezers carefully removing a sharp splinter.

"I remember times when my grandfather, after going to a special cupboard and getting out a tin container of herbal salve, would hold my hand and tell me everything was going to be okay," shares my friend Martha, now a grandmother. "Then he would remove some of the strong-smelling ointment and apply it to my ridiculously tiny wound."

Martha can still recall the folk remedy's immediate effect. "No matter how small the scrape," she reflects, "his kindness made me feel so much better."

"My grandma's miracle cure was something called Mentholatum," reminisces Tom, a forty-eight year old public administrator and the grandfather of a two year old. "She used that stuff for everything. We ate it, drank it, slept with it—probably even took baths in it. Looking back, I'm not even sure that it was safe!"

Thankfully, most grandparents today are not likely to use dubious remedies or self-concocted (and potentially toxic) medical compounds when it is time to treat family ailments. But there is one thing about our grandparents' medicinal ministrations that we will undoubtedly pass along to the next generation: the special brand of TLC, available only from Grandpa or Grandma, that eases discomfort and assists healing.

> *Love is a fruit in season at all times.*
> Mother Teresa, *Heart of Joy*

With a wide variety of safe and effective treatments to choose from, we can quickly gain confidence in our ability to manage most minor emergencies and illnesses at home.

The number one worry about temporarily caring for grandchildren, for most grandparents, is the danger of accidental injury, and with good reason: accidents are the leading cause of death among children in the United States.

After reviewing this chapter, taking CPR training, buying and reading a children's first aid manual, putting together a first-aid kit, and childproofing your yard and house, you will be well-prepared to promote and protect your grandchild's health and safety.

First-Aid Supplies

As your grandchild grows, you will want to keep a well stocked first-aid supply box on hand, just in case. A list of all your first-aid kit should contain is found in Additional Resources, page 199. All items on this list are available at your local drugstore. Make your kit distinctive: decorate it with bright-colored markers, pictures, or humorous wrapping paper.

Though it is unlikely that you will ever need it, it is wise to have a medical emergency consent form. Be sure to have one on hand—filled out, signed, and in an easy-to-locate spot—whenever your grandchild is with you and his parents are difficult to reach. The following sample can be adapted as appropriate to fit your family's needs.

Medical Emergency Consent Form

We, the undersigned parents of

_____ (child's name), a

minor, do hereby authorize _____

(grandparent's name) as our agent to consent to any

emergency medical treatment in our absence. This

authorization shall remain effective until date unless sooner

revoked in writing.

    My child's physician, address and phone number are

_____

_____ .

    Our insurance company and policy number are

_____

_____ .

    My child's special health concerns list of known

allergies and conditions_____

_____

_____

_____ .

    The date of my child's last tetanus booster was

_____ .

    The parents agree to hold harmless the person

appointed and the physician providing treatment from and

against any and all loss, damage, expense, and costs of any

kind arising out of or in connection with that person's or

physician's acting in reliance upon the authorization set

herein, with the exception of actions which amount to

gross negligence. The physician shall not be relieved on the

basis of this authorization from liability for negligence in

the diagnosis and treatment of a minor.

    Signature _____ Date_____

    Witness _____Date_____

Caring for a Child with a Fever

In case your grandchild develops (or already has) a fever when he is staying with you, you should review the following information.

Each child reacts differently to fever-producing ailments. Some will "spike" a high fever in the absence of serious sickness; others experience only a slight temperature rise after developing a full-blown infection. Your degree of worry should depend on how sick your grandchild acts, not on the thermometer's numerical reading alone. Ask your grandchild's parents to tell you what degree of temperature they want you to be concerned about.

Watch for signs of improvement. If your grandchild responds normally to you, is active and wants to play, or is smiling, alert, and involved in what is going on, you will know that he is feeling better.

If, on the other hand, your grandchild is acting increasingly sicker—drowsy, lethargic, unresponsive, or just lying around with little movement, his parents (or the doctor, in their absence) should be called. Are there any new symptoms to be concerned about, such as earache, severe cough, skin rash, sore throat, painful urination, or abdominal pain? Have you noticed that your grandchild acts sick even when the fever comes down after the application of a fever reliever? A "yes" answer to any of these questions means you should check in with the parents or doctor.

In treating the fever, you will probably be instructed to do the following: take the baby's temperature (if you have not already done this); give acetaminophen every three to four hours according to the recommended dose; provide extra fluids frequently (about ten percent more fluids for each degree Fahrenheit of temperature elevation); and cool the baby down by using a fan, lowering the room temperature; and avoiding too many clothes and blankets.

Soothe your grandchild with your loving touch and quiet presence. When your grandchild is not feeling well, you will want to reassure him that "Grandma's here" by staying close by as much as possible. Rocking, back rubs, or just sitting by his bed will let him know he is not alone—he has you to pray and care for him. And that's some of the best medicine of all.

When You Need to Give Medicine

Sooner or later, you will most likely be called upon to give medicine to your grandchild. Here is what you should know.

Know about the medicine you are giving. Before you give the medicine, be sure to find out what it is and if there are any adverse reactions to watch for.

Ask the following questions about the medicine: What kind of medicine is it? How should it be stored? Should the medicine be given with meals or on an empty stomach? Are there foods your grandchild needs to avoid while on this medicine? How is it measured?

Do you understand the instructions? Write down and closely follow all instructions about the medicine, including how often and how much of the medicine you will give.

Check special labels. Some medicine containers have labels to remind you of special instructions about shaking, timing, avoiding sunlight, or other concerns. Be sure you understand what these mean, and apply the information carefully.

Measure accurately. Use a specially marked (calibrated) spoon or dropper to measure liquid medicine, making sure to measure the amount as accurately as you possibly can.

Don't be dishonest. In other words, don't tell your grandchild the medicine tastes good if it tastes bad. If he has already had it, he will know you're not telling the truth; if he has not had it yet, he will know you're not telling the truth as soon as he takes the medicine.

There are three things you should never do when giving medicine:

—Never give your grandchild medicine intended for someone else.

—Never give medicine after the expiration date has passed.

—Never tell your grandchild that the medicine is candy.

What to Do in Case of Accidental Poisoning

The very thought of your grandchild ingesting poison is enough to stop you cold—but remember these facts. First, most poisonings can be prevented by keeping all poisonous substances in their original containers and out of children's reach (behind childproof latched doors or in high cabinets) at all times. For a list of poisonous plants and household substances, see Additional Resources, pages 201-203.

Secondly, should accidental poisoning occur, quick first-aid and professional help are your best defense against lasting harm. In such a situation, follow this advice:

Stay calm—don't panic.

All cases of poisoning require professional medical attention. Call 911 or your local poison control center or physician immediately and get advice on what to do. Give the center this information:

—Name of the substance ingested

—List of ingredients, if available

—Time and suspected amount of ingestion

—Age and weight of child

Attempt to identify the poisonous substance without undue delay. Save the container, if possible; take it with you to the emergency room. The ingested substance must be identified before therapy can be started. Children who are unconscious or have swallowed a strong alkali require admission to the hospital.

Although poisons may be inhaled or absorbed through the skin, swallowing (called oral poisoning) is the most common route of entry. There are two types of first-aid treatment for oral poisoning: those in which vomiting should be induced, and those in which it should not.

Do not induce vomiting if your grandchild has swallowed an acid (battery acid, bleach, hair straightener, etc.), an alkali (Drano or other drain cleaner, oven cleaner, etc.), or a petroleum product (gasoline, lighter fluid, kerosene, etc.). In these cases, give milk to neutralize the substance while obtaining emergency medical help. If you don't have milk, give water or milk of magnesia instead.

Vomiting is usually recommended to remove most medications and poisonous plants. If you are directed to induce vomiting, remember: it's a safe and effective remedy in many cases. When indicated, the stomach will be evacuated by suction during medical treatment.

Vomiting may be induced by stimulating the back of the child's throat with your finger, or by giving two to four teaspoons of syrup (not extract) of ipecac, followed by as much liquid as he or she will drink. Or you can try both. (Mustard mixed with warm water also works.) Collect the vomit in a plastic bag to be examined later by a physician.

If there is no vomiting within twenty-five minutes, repeat the dose of syrup of ipecac.

After home treatment is applied, follow-up by phone or at a physician's office will probably be recommended.

Obtaining Immediate Medical Help

When making a call to obtain emergency medical services, be ready to give the dispatcher your address or present location, including directions when necessary, your phone number, the child's name, age, condition, and cause of condition.

The following conditions require immediate emergency care:

Major injury. Possible back or neck injury, complicated fractures, or a large chest wound are examples of the kind of medical trauma best treated by emergency medical technicians. Do not move the child if you suspect internal trauma is present or think ambulance transfer will be safest.

Choking. If an object becomes lodged in your grandchild's windpipe and first-aid techniques fail, call EMS immediately. Signs to look for: gasping, gagging, coughing, wheezing, fainting, or face turning blue.

Coma or unconsciousness. A severe allergic reaction, poisoning, drowning, electric shock, or head trauma can rapidly cause unconsciousness. If the child's breathing and/or heart stops, begin artificial respiration (and CPR, if needed) immediately while someone calls EMS.

Heavy bleeding (hemorrhage). Cuts that produce pulsing, vigorous bleeding require immediate EMS attention. If significant blood loss exists and you can't stop the bleeding by direct pressure, call an ambulance at once—because of their smaller body size, children cannot tolerate as much blood loss as adults can.

Sharing Yourself with
Your Grandchildren

9
Staying Close, No Matter What

Still-steaming sit-down meals on Sunday after church. Annual holiday celebrations. Ripe, red strawberries from Grandma's garden. Picnics by the lake. Extended family get-togethers at the cabin. Grandpa's Fourth of July campfire and fireworks extravaganza. Birthday cake with brightly colored candles and Neapolitan ice cream.

Today's hectic pace creates a longing to recreate our cherished childhood memories, the times when family sharing took place at a slower pace, with fewer distractions. I remember peering at the sky from Grandma McMahon's hammock and singing in Grandma Allen's porch swing. No one ever seemed to be in a hurry. Somehow, as if by magic, a fresh-from-the-oven apple or cherry pie often appeared on the table after dinner—clear evidence of a grandmother's afternoon labor. Looking back, I can see that my child eyes held a limited range of vision.

The power of our memories and of the past is part of what makes grandparents unique: we introduce our children's children to previous generations' traditions and to our family's distinctive ways.

Love has good manners and does not pursue selfish advantage. It is not touchy. It does not keep account of evil or gloat over the wickedness of other people. On the contrary, it shares the joy of those who live by the truth.
1 Corinthians 13:5, 6
(PH)

We form the link to their own parents' childhood heritage.

Being a grandparent presents a one-of-a-kind opportunity for us to share the best part of our lives with our grandchildren, to take time out from the hectic pace of life and set aside quiet moments for sharing our skills with a new generation. "Your greatest danger is letting the urgent things crowd out the important," writes Charles E. Hummel in *Tyranny of the Urgent*.[1] With a grandchild at one's side, even simple things take on great importance: picking flowers, baking cookies, going for a walk, cleaning out a closet, fixing a bicycle, gazing at the stars.

Our grandchildren are not the only ones who benefit from joining us on our everyday excursions. Children have much to teach us by their thoughtful insights, remarks, questions, and replies. When they are missing from our lives, a void is created for both generations. But when we make room for this special, side-by-side relationship, exciting things happen. Life takes on greater meaning. Priorities are rearranged in the family's favor. An enduring bond develops that will last beyond our lifetime.

Building the Bond

The grandparent-grandchild relationship is nurtured by sharing experiences and spending time with each other. It's a simple formula for success, really: As we focus caring attention on our grandchildren, our grandchildren reward us with love, humor, enthusiasm, and affection in return. We can afford to be more easygoing and relaxed, to enjoy one another's presence, because we do not carry the daily burden of parenting responsibilities.

We have greater stamina to go beyond the basics. We provide the extras. We add the distinctive little details.

"A grandparent serves many purposes for the child, which no parent can fulfill," explains pediatrician Dr. T. Berry Brazelton in *Families: Crisis and Caring*. "A long history of exposure to grandparents gives children a chance both to absorb and to test out the strengths, principles, and beliefs that characterize each family."[2]

To those of us who wonder how to make ourselves important to our grandchildren—and useful to our children—Dr. Brazelton[3] suggests:

Stick up for our unique role. By assuming a role that bestows approval, expresses loving delight in the child, and offers consistent support for the parents, we assure that both generations will welcome our committed, ongoing involvement.

Offer to sit regularly, at a time when they need us. Whether we babysit on a weekly basis, just once in a while, or every day, parents will appreciate our help. They know they can relax—for an evening out, a leisurely afternoon away from the house, or an entire weekend—while we supply some relief.

Provide the focus and the means for holiday reunions. In today's extended families, substantial effort and energy are required to bring everyone together for annual holiday celebrations. But the results are well worth the investment. By emphasizing fun and family traditions over headache-producing hassles (housing several families under one roof for a few days, organizing and preparing meals for a large group, making complicated travel arrangements, keeping the house manageably clean), we bring family-oriented continuity and lasting meaning to our loved ones' lives.

Make rituals out of our meetings with our grandchildren. Talking about family history; giving "I was thinking of you today" presents (especially something the child collects, such as a pack of baseball cards, Legos, or an unusual set of stickers); going on special outings to the zoo, science center, children's museum, library, or neighborhood park; and reading a good book create special memories that strengthen our bond when we are together.

Offer both generations an emotional sanctuary and stability. Put simply, this means that we will choose to stay quiet when we might prefer to give advice. "Grandparents no longer need to be parents, nor are they teachers," Dr. Brazelton wisely reminds us. "That's the lovely freedom of the role. Just sit and rock in the midst of chaos. Let them come to you. You can offer comfort, family love, experience, hugs, and a sense of strength and stability for each member of the family. Parents must be the disciplinarians. Teaching, in a direct sense, is better left to them and to teachers. You can offer children a sense of family customs and wisdom when they ask for it. They will be learning from you whenever they are with you, by example, . . . Be the person you want them to remember."[4]

Avoid rushing up to young children, unless we want them to withdraw. Instead, we can look past the child toward his parent, perhaps holding a toy out, and wait for the child to show interest in us. Dr. Brazelton cautions grandparents never to grab a child out of his parents' arms—"the safety of those arms is too critical," he says—and to "speak gently," without staring in his face. As the child's anxiety lessens, it is a signal to move in closer. Over time, as grandchildren become well-acquainted with their grandparents, these concerns vanish.

> *A grandparent will help you with your buttons, your zippers, and your shoelaces and not be in any hurry for you to grow up.*
> Erma Bombeck

Keep involved when we live far away. Phone calls, presents, letters, videotapes, and regular, short visits are great ways to stay in touch. Don't let the miles prevent you from taking part in the grit and glory of grandparenting joys. (A more detailed discussion of long-distance grandparenting is found later in this chapter.)

Unconditional Love

Children who enjoy a close relationship with their grandparents reap a number of significant benefits, including a wonderful sense that "there is someone out there who loves me very much, no matter what, just for being me." Our grandchildren do not have to prove their lovability to us; we love them regardless of their personal attributes and achievements. We cherish their lives as a precious gift and marvel at their existence—just the fact that they are here.

Putting our feelings into words is not always easy or automatic.

50 AFFIRMING STATEMENTS

Affirmations for Being

I love you.

I think you're a neat boy (or girl).

I enjoy you.

I'm glad you came over today.

I like to hug you.

I'm glad God made you a girl (or I'm glad you're a boy).

I'm happy to see you!

Don't pay any attention to them, (child's name). You'll walk when you're ready.

Your needs are okay with me.

I'm thinking about you today.

I'm glad you're my grandchild.

Are you hungry now? Okay—I'll get you some food.

Your diapers are wet. I'll change you.

I like the way you look.

You are unique.

Hello, (child's name)! It's great to have you here.

I'm glad we're doing this (name activity) together.

I like to sit by you.

You're a joy!

Affirmations for Doing

I like the way you did that, (child's name).

You did a nice job with that!

What you're doing is really interesting.

You do neat work, (child's name).

Go ahead and try that. If it doesn't work, that's okay.

What are you doing there, honey? Oh, I see now. That's much better. Keep it up.

I enjoy watching you . . . (build with your blocks, play piano, make a drawing, etc.).

Nice job, (child's name)!

You can have my full attention without . . . (making messes, whining, spilling milk, etc.)

You can ask for help when you need it.

Affirmations for Thinking

You made a smart decision, (child's name).

115

Let me know what you need.

You look mad, (child's name)! I'm here to help.

I'm not afraid of your anger.

Think about what you need and tell me.

Don't do this (name behavior), because (provide reason); do this (give alternative) instead.

You figured out how to do that (name specific accomplishment) very well.

It's okay to feel mad, but I won't let you. . . (hurt your brother, break the dish, etc.)

That scared me when I was your age, too. Let's think about what we can do.

I enjoy seeing you grow up and learn new things.

Affirmations for Identity

(three to six years)

You don't have to act sad (or sick or mad or scary) to get taken care of.

When you stop whining and tell me what you need, I'll help you.

You can tell me how you feel.

I love you, (child's name).

What do you think about that?

Thank you for cooperating with me, (child's name).

That funny dog really likes you—you really know how to pet her.

I'll appreciate your help with (name activity), (child's name).

I liked the way you gave your sister some of your sports cards. That was very nice of you!

Watch what happens next in the basketball game and tell me how you think it's going to turn out.

10 Affirming Actions

Listening

Nurturing touch: kissing, hugging, patting (if acceptable to your grandchild)

Calling your grandchild by name

Smiling

One-on-one time

Sending a letter

Spending time together

Taking your grandchild to do something he enjoys

Calling by phone just to say hello

Celebrating an accomplishment or your grandchild's special day [5]

When we became parents, we learned about how to communicate with our children along the way. Now that we are grandparents, we have been given another opportunity to affirm a new generation of children.

See the lists on pages 115-116 for a variety of affirmations we can use with our grandchildren—affirming who they are, what they do, what they think about, and how they view themselves.

Long-distance Grandparenting

"Grandma, do you have to go?" Four-year-old Sarah gently placed her small hand on her grandmother's shoulder as they sat together near Gate 9, waiting for the flight to begin boarding.

"Sarah, Grandma lives in Tucson, Arizona. Do you remember visiting with her there last year when we flew down for Thanksgiving?" her mom calmly asked. "She can't stay with us because that's where she lives. Our house is in Michigan—a long way from Arizona."

"But why do we live so far away from each other?"

Long-distance grandparenting is a fact of life for many of us. Although a fair percentage of people still live in (or near) the county where they grew up, millions have moved away from their home-towns—permanently. And a good number of us find ourselves undergoing regular relocations.

Uprooted and repotted, we go where our jobs, ministries, schooling, natures, or condominiums call us, periodically transplanting our lives somewhere over the distant horizon. The problem is, our adult children and grandchildren cannot pull up their stakes every time we do. Often, they are the ones who choose to move. As a result, we can eventually end up living thousands of miles apart from each other.

But a healthy grandparent-grandchild bond thrives on person-to-person contact, not traumatic separations. How can we minimize what we've lost?

There is no denying that the ideal situation, in many cases, is for grandparents to live close to their grandchildren—no farther away than a day's drive. Yet this is not always possible.

No matter what geographic distance exists between our families, we can remain close to our grandchildren, in spite of the miles. We can continue to play an important role in our grandchildren's lives,

> *Grandparents show children the mountaintops, while parents must teach the drudgeries of how to get there.*
> Dr. T. Berry Brazelton,
> *Families: Crisis & Caring*

believing that the irreplaceable bond we share is strong and durable. We can remain involved by giving our grandchildren unconditional love and caring affirmations— through phone calls, mail packages, audio- and videotapes, and family newsletters. And we can refuse to let the distance diminish our capacity for active demonstrations of affection.

"What is important is the consistency and the reliability of your connection," grandparenting expert Dr. Arthur Kornhaber points out in *Grandparent Power!* "The children will flourish if they know they can count on hearing from you and seeing you, even infrequently, but on a predictable basis.

"In fact, there is one aspect of long-distance grandparenting that is quite positive. Your visits, when you do manage to get together, will be intensely meaningful and exciting for everyone concerned. There is a certain romance to looking forward to being with those you love, plus a heightened sense of how special you are to one another."

He adds, "There is also, to be sure, the fresh grief that comes with saying good-bye at the end of each visit, but even that, as life experiences go, is more positive than negative. It underscores how much you care about one another."[6]

Sight & Sound

When we live apart, we need to do more, not less, to support and stay in close touch with our grandchildren. The following suggestions will encourage you in this direction.

Record songs, rhymes, and read-aloud stories. Start by sharing your favorites and talk to your grandchild throughout the recording. Lullabies for little ones, including those you sang to your children when they were tiny tots, will be especially treasured.

Rhythmical nursery rhymes are fun to both read and listen to. Children's praise songs, accompanied by guitar or piano if you have

IDEAS FOR STAYING CLOSE

Keep a notebook handy for jotting down things that you want to talk about with your grandchild.

Start a hobby or collection together, periodically adding new items to your grandchild's assortment; stay updated by phone calls or writing letters.

Enclose stamps, prepaid postcards, and self-addressed, stamped envelopes with a packet of stationery, ink pad, rubber stamp, and stickers to encourage letter writing.

Time your phone calls when the rates are lowest; subscribe to a long-distance carrier with liberal "night-rate" hours, free holiday phone calls, or other special discounts.

Send greeting cards when you don't have extra time to write a letter.

Clip pictures, cartoons, and articles for your grandchild's enjoyment; encourage ongoing communication by sticking to the subjects he is interested in.

Stock up on colorful postcards for sending quick notes.

Mail taped messages back and forth when you cannot afford long-distance phone calls.

Play a game—checkers or chess, for example—by mail.

Watch a sporting event or television show together over the phone.

Give your grandchild a scrapbook "just like Grandma's"; make duplicate copies of each item and regularly send packets to each other.

Share recipes: bake samples and send by priority mail; tuck a copy of the recipe inside the box.

one, make an especially appealing tape. Your local Christian bookseller will be happy to help you locate the appropriate music books.

If you are unfamiliar with children's literature, browse through a recommended-reading overview. You may want to discuss your selections with your grandchild's parent before you begin making the recording. As you read, do not be surprised if you find yourself returning on your own exciting adventure to Aslan's Narnia, Pooh Corner, and Mr. MacGregor's farm.

Practice reading the book through aloud before you record on tape. Try getting into the character as you read dialogue: the more varied your "voices" are, the more interesting the tape will be. The same advice applies to reading Bible stories.

When possible, mail picture books along with the cassette tape for your grandchild's added enjoyment. (Helpful hint: borrowed public books, when returned directly to their source, may be mailed back at the less-expensive "library rate"—be sure to include the due date with the book.)

Video a visit. Given the wide availability of video cameras, VCRs, and two-day priority mail service, why limit your visits to infrequent face-to-face encounters? It is so much fun to see Grandma or Grandpa talking on the television, especially when the visit includes favorite sights and sounds: an interview with the family pet, photo album reviews, funny music concerts, worship services, or holiday remembrances. The number of potential scripts and subjects you can create are virtually unlimited.

As an added bonus, your video visits will help establish a permanent family record for future generations to take delight in. Best of all, the videos you create will be available for your current grandchildren to "visit" with you whenever they want.

Vary locations to keep things interesting—for example, Gramps weeding his herb garden or Gram working at the computer. Tape favorite activities that your grandchild will enjoy watching, such as baking chocolate chip cookies (with a box of the homemade treats tucked next to the video), working on a project in the garage, hunting for antiques, running in a marathon, taking a train ride, going for a walk at the beach, visiting the zoo, driving by familiar spots around town, and sightseeing out-of-state. The list of potential sites and activities is truly phenomenal.

If your children own a video camera, ask them to make you a "highlight" tape from your grandchild's day, and encourage them to frequently share copies of their own videos with you.

Phone just to talk—and listen. Regular phone visits provide "the next best thing" to an in-person, two-way encounter with your grandchild. Once your grandchild can make even a few sounds, ask your child to put him on the phone. These memorable interactions aren't a replacement for the real thing, of course, but if you call regularly for the dual purpose of honoring your grandchild's one-of-a-kind identity and building up your special bond, you will both reap the benefits. Budget accordingly.

> *Be joyful in hope, patient in affliction, faithful in prayer. Share with God's people who are in need. Practice hospitality.*
> Romans 12:12

Some long-distance phone companies offer significant family discounts on calls placed between 5 PM and 8 AM, as well as all day on Saturday and for most of Sunday. In addition, at least one long-distance carrier allows free unlimited calling to listed family members on major holidays.

Telephone to commemorate both large and small triumphs. And call to listen. What's the best thing that happened in David's life today? Is there a special event he's looking forward to attending? How are the Atlanta Braves doing in the play-offs this week? Consider offering your children the use of a toll-free "call home" number so that they may call to fill you in on your grandchild's latest experiences.

By picking up on your grandchild's likes and dislikes early on, and keeping up-to-date on his interests, your conversations won't tend to be repetitious or boring. Because you are really listening, he will know that he can talk about his life with you and you won't discount the importance of his observations and opinions. Don't you wish your grandparents had done this with you?

Reading & Writing

Create a family newsletter. Why wait for the annual Christmas letter to collectively celebrate your clan's accomplishments?

Kids of all ages like to see their names in print and read about themselves, at any time of year. Call for submissions from family members—drawings, photos, articles, poems, calendars, book and movie reviews, upcoming events, announcements—then publish and mail out the missives on a weekly, biweekly, or monthly basis. Or bimonthly or quarterly updates, if that is what your schedule requires.

Make it as simple or elaborate as you wish. (Remember "The Pickwick Portfolio" in Louisa May Alcott's *Little Women?*) Even headlines like "Jon Advances to Second Chair Tuba" or "Katy Finds

Lost Wallet" entertain children, in addition to providing them with a little extra encouragement to spend some time reading.

You do not have to be an expert in desktop publishing to print a newsletter your family will derive enjoyment from: all you need is a pen or typewriter and a commercial photocopier to achieve satisfying results.

Attach notes to interesting artifacts. Children love receiving mail. But they love it even more when it's accompanied by stickers, cartoons, coloring books, collector's cards, puzzles, paper dolls, personalized memo pads, vintage hankies, pencil sets, or a teddy bear blanket. Let's face it—with young kids, small surprises speak louder than words, and it is easy to add just a little something extra in the envelope for only a few cents more.

Handwritten letters highlighted with colored pens and markers will lend interest to printed sentiments. Decorate the paper by gluing on bright colored fabric strips, ribbon pieces, or leftover gift wrap scraps. Doodles are definitely to be indulged in. Use you own unique symbol—like a circular face with a quirky smile, star-shaped earrings, and your own distinctive hairstyle—as an added signature for a toddler who can't read.

One grandma says, "After my granddaughter, Olivia, was born, it was really hard to leave her when the time came for me to return home. So, even though she couldn't read yet, I started to write letters to her—anecdotes about our family, descriptions of interesting events, my memories of my granddaughter's arrival. I asked my daughter-in-law to read them to her later, when Olivia is able to understand them."

Exchange E-mail and/or faxes. Your grandchild might be more proficient with his PC than you are, but who cares? Once you understand how it works and coordinate your on-line services, you will find that E-mail is faster and, after you get the hang of it, easier than handwriting a letter—and your grandchild will be happy to find your notes waiting in her personal mailbox.

Sending a fax is another quick way to send something of interest to your grandchild. Can you imagine what it would have been like to

122

receive a copy of your grandmother's handwritten cherry cobbler recipe, including juice stains, after leaving a message on her answering machine that you wanted to make the special dessert for tonight's dinner?

Note: You can fax at any time, without interrupting your child's family, when you see something you want to share. And they can do the same with you.

Well-planned Visits

Schedule regular, short stays. Three to four days may be the best. Unless there is a specific reason to stay for a longer period of time—to help out during a parent's hospital stay, after a new baby's arrival, or when the parents will be vacationing alone, for example—plan a brief visit to keep stress at a minimum.

Make necessary arrangements in advance. When possible, set up your travel reservations and organize transportation to and from the airport ahead of time. Consider staying in a conveniently located hotel, bed-and-breakfast, or residential suite during an extended stay if you desire privacy on your vacation; if there is a swimming pool, your grandchildren may enjoy "getting away," too. For an in-house stay with your children and grandchildren, discuss your needs and expectations in advance, and ask them to give you their suggestions about how you can fit in comfortably with their daily routines.

Consider yourself a guest while staying in your children's home. Do not expect your kids to rearrange their schedules, banish the pets to the backyard, or give up their bed just because you have traveled a great distance for the visit. Find ways to fit in without disrupting their too-hectic lives. Take along things to do for when they—and you— need a break: reading and writing materials, needlework, recreational clothing and equipment, your laptop computer. Plan activities that take their schedules and preferences into consideration. And, above all, be flexible.

Keep your goals in mind. Your primary

> *Who would want trials and difficulties? You command us to endure them, not to love them.*
> Augustine of Hippo

reason for visiting is to spend time with your children and grandchildren. Before you know it, you will be back at home and back to your normal routines and daily schedule. Stay focused on the positive—enjoy your grandchildren to the fullest while you are there. Have fun!

Facing Family Changes

One of the greatest gifts we can offer our children is to serve as a backup system and a safety net in the face of family change and crisis. Our love, prayers, practical support, and willingness to listen—to "be there" for them—brings a sense of stability and continuity during difficult life transitions. And this, in turn, benefits our grandchildren.

Too often, marriages end in divorce; unemployment hits without warning; frequent relocations produce emotional trauma. How will we respond if our grandchildren become affected by these things?

When Your Child Divorces

"I knew the numbers: More than two million divorces occur in the United States every year. I just didn't think it would happen to one of my kids," Jane shared with me. "What did I do wrong?"

Jane's question is one of the first thoughts that many parents have when they are told about their children's impending marital breakup. Feeling angry and wondering what more you might have done to avert the divorce, it seems only reasonable to blame someone for what has happened.

Shock, denial, anger, guilt, and a feeling of powerlessness over the situation are a normal part of mourning a child's divorce. During this unpredictable and erratic grief process, you may find yourself often thinking, "This can't be happening" or "If only I had . . ." or "Why won't they just work it out?" Then reality sets in. The marriage is over. Your grandchildren's mom and dad will never live

> *A child's hand in yours—what tenderness and power it arouses. You are instantly the very touchstone of wisdom and strength.*
> Marjorie Holmes

under the same roof again. The relationship you share with your in-law has been permanently altered.

"Divorce dramatically and quickly changes the role of grand-parents, so naturally they will have their own adjustments to make," writer Vicki Lansky informs couples in *Vicki Lansky's Divorce Book for Parents.* "Sometimes they are called upon for financial aid, for temporary housing, for baby-sitting services, and are expected to give advice only when asked for it. Grandchildren may disappear from their lives or take over their lives. Your divorce is not just your divorce—it's theirs, too."[7]

As a grandparent, there are plenty of good reasons to maintain a loving and secure bond with your grandchildren after their parents divorce. "The perfect grandparents give kids a sense of continuity and the awareness of belonging to a large and interesting family," Lansky points out. "They're always available to love a child and to listen, and kids sometimes find it easier to confide in them than a parent. The elders can also fill in for an absent parent, giving him or her the gift of time off without worry."[8]

Studies have shown that grandparents' caring involvement in the aftermath of divorce has a consoling effect on their grandchildren, in addition to providing some relief for their distressed parents.

"Grandparents are the link with the past that gives children the sense that the family was here before and will continue to thrive," say Dorothy Weiss Gottlieb, Inez Bellow Gottlieb, and Marjorie A. Slavin, authors of *What to Do When Your Son or Daughter Divorces.*[9]

"You are keenly aware that as you reach out to your grandchildren they are getting something unique that they don't receive from any other people in their lives."[10]

To maintain your bond and facilitate the healing process, they recommend that you:

Allow yourself to grieve. Realize that the early months of the divorce process are the hardest. At first, you may want to withdraw from your child's family to protect yourself from the emotional pain you are experiencing. That's understandable. You will encounter a wide range of feelings as you work through your family's loss, and the desire to "just get on with life" by pulling back on your involvement is a natural one. Keep in mind, however, that your grandchildren may not be able to understand this reaction. Reassure them that your love remains constant.

Avoid taking sides. Be available to listen to your grandchild's concerns. Find out from your child how the divorce has been explained and if there are any areas that he or she doesn't want discussed. Take your grandchild's age into consideration during your conversations. Keep your comments and explanations as simple as possible.

The way things are going today is not how things will be going a few years down the road, or even six months from now. Because your child is more likely to ask for help sooner than later, remember that your current level of support does not automatically set a precedent for the future. Discuss your concerns and expectations up front, when possible, to avoid future misunderstandings.

Don't take it personally if your grandchild temporarily loses interest in sharing activities you once enjoyed together. Your grief-stricken grandchild may find social interactions difficult for now. But this does not mean that you should pull back entirely—keep reaching out. Be willing to accept no for an answer, and avoid attempts at pleading and persuasion. In time, your grandchild will say "Yes" again. When she does, plan low-key activities that are relaxing, simple, and fun.

If your child has custody of your grandchildren, your relationship is less likely to be affected by the divorce than if you are on the noncustodial side of the decree. If your in-law is restricting contact with your grandchildren, remember that it may be a short-lived reaction. Stay in touch to demonstrate your love and concern; remain available to your grandchildren by telephone and written communication. Be persistent in expressing your intent to continue to play an important role in your grandchildren's lives.

Realize that your grandchild is likely to regress. Expect your grandchild to behave a good deal younger than he is—up to half his actual age. This is an important time for you to provide loving, one-way support, without expecting your grandchild to reward you, or behave according to your wishes, in return. Let your strong love be a reliable covering.

Seek legal visitation rights, if necessary. Today, all states have laws addressing the grandparent's right to child visitation. But these laws do not automatically guarantee that you will be able to see or talk with your grandchild. If the custodial parent denies visitation, you must legally prove why it is in the child's best interest to remain in contact with you. To avoid this possibility, ask your child to request visitation rights for you as part of the divorce settlement. If this is unsuccessful, try using mediation—a less expensive and, usually, more effective alternative to courtroom conflict. For additional support and information, contact a grandparents' visitation rights organization. (See Additional Resources, page 206.)

When Your Child Wants to Return Home

A recent feature article in our local paper, the *Austin-American Statesman*, began like this.

Mary Wright, 47, thought she was done with kids. Her children did what she expected: moved out, got married, had their own kids. She bought a roomy new house perfect for one, comfortable and quiet. (Emphasis on quiet.) Then son Chris, a single father, moved in with his three young children.

"I had order in my life. It was peaceful, and I had everything under control," Wright recalls.

Life has changed.

She's dealing with issues she hadn't thought of in years: weaning babies from the bottle, potty training, chicken pox (all three kids in a row) and the first day of school. The situation is not unique. A growing number of grandparents are taking active roles in raising grandchildren, and some of them are the sole providers.

"People tell me, 'I can't believe you're doing that.' I tell them

I did what I had to do," says Wright.

Make no mistake. She did it out of love.[11]

Divorce is just one of the reasons adult children return to their parents' homes. The loss of a job, domestic abuse, serious illness, financial crisis, or desire for a temporary living arrangement due to a sudden relocation, full-time schooling, or building a new house may also find you being asked to open your doors to your child's family.

This should not be surprising. Home represents refuge, and as such, can be a safe haven for our children to return to when things don't go the way they—or, for that matter, we—had planned. The question is, will we regret saying, "Yes, come on in" in the days, weeks, or even months, after our kids move in?

There is no denying that your life has changed since your adult child moved out and established a home of her or his own. Your daily routines, work schedule, and personal interests have changed dramatically in recent years. Like Mary Wright, you thought you "were done with kids." You may be unwilling to accommodate the necessary changes that would make the alternative living arrangement feasible. Counting the costs ahead of time, even if it means the answer is "No," is essential if you want to avoid future conflict.

Develop a plan with your child, using these questions as a guide:

How long will you be staying?

How much will you be paying for your share of the expenses?

How will we resolve disputes and reconcile schedule conflicts?

How will you treat my house?

How will we handle meals, phone calls, visitors, mail deliveries, and so on?

Only you can know whether inviting your child and his or her family to stay with you is something that will be beneficial to everyone involved, given "the big picture" of your current situation. Although it won't be easy, the choice to temporarily share your home can be well worth the effort required when you know that it is the right thing to do for now.

When You Are a Single Grandparent

Being a single grandparent was never part of your dream. Your long-range goal was to remain with your husband for life—through a relatively smooth succession of years spent working, bearing children, parenting, empty-nesting, grandparenting, and then retiring together. You never imagined that your family would be permanently split apart by death or divorce. But somewhere along the way, your marriage ideal no longer fit.

With the arrival of the next generation, you may experience renewed grief and disappointment about making the journey alone. As a single grandparent, you may find yourself in the midst of rebuilding your own life when your first grandchild arrives.

The birth of a grandchild, though a joyous event, is also a strong reminder that you are growing older. Welcoming this new dimension of your life does not mean that you will not feel ambivalent about becoming a grandparent. Making peace with your new status will mean confronting your own inner conflict. Be patient with yourself as you accept, adjust, and adapt. In time, you may find that grand-parenting offers you a heart-expanding relationship unlike any you have experienced.

On the other hand, becoming a grandparent may be something you have looked forward to for a long time—an amazing triumph that has brought a deep sense of meaning and value to your family role. You have found that active participation in your grandchild's life has expanded, instead of limited, your horizons. Seeing your grandchild's face light up when you walk into a room gives you the kind of lasting satisfaction that other people's praise and compliments cannot provide.

"I treasure each and every one of my grandchildren's hugs and smiles," my widowed mother-in-law, Elizabeth Evans, once told me. "I am very rich." Though Mom worked full-time and carried on an active social life apart from her children's families, she placed a high priority on spending time with her grandchildren. When she remarried, her second husband was included in the family circle after instantly becoming a grandfather of six children, age five and under. Through the years, my husband, Dave, and I deeply appreciated their caring involvement with our growing family. The bonds shared by three generations benefited all of us as we found ways to fit in with each other's changing life seasons.

10
Making Memories Together

Our busy lives are brimful of activity. Competing demands tend to crowd out the "optional" in favor of the "necessary"; former family traditions may fall by the wayside. To preserve the happy portions of our heritage, we must sort through our priorities and thoughtfully consider which family traditions we wish to pass on to our grandchildren.

"People's fondest memories of family life are typically nothing really complicated or expensive activities," explains Dr. Nick Stinnett in *Family Building*. "They remember such things as eating meals together, going to an uncle's house together, or enjoying Dad pulling them on a sled. The common thread is simply doing some things together that were enjoyable. The activities are not all entertainment; they include work, too."

Dr. Stinnett's extensive study of three thousand American families has led him to conclude: "Strong families do a lot of activities together. They spend a great deal of time together. They work together, play together, go places together, and eat together. . . they are as busy as you and I or anybody else. But they make their family life a top priority with respect to the way they spend their time."[1]

In this chapter, you will find loads of ideas for strengthening your family through creating family memories with your grandchildren, including practical suggestions for making once-in-a-while festive occasions, annual celebrations, and holiday traditions events that each child will look forward to—and later, look back on—with joy.

Birthdays: Making Your Grandchild's Day Special

There's only one really important message to send and celebrate on your grandchild's birthday— "I'm glad you were born!" It's a day for affirming and appreciating the child's God-given identity and how happy you are that he is alive. Here are just a few ideas.

"Just-me-and-you" birthday outing. Take your grandchild out separately to buy his birthday gift in a specified price range, then share a meal or a snack at a favorite restaurant.

Hang up a birthday banner. Buy a roll of white banner paper (or a commercially made banner), then decorate it with an extra-wide marking pen; place it above the front door or in another prominent place. Adorn the banner with ribbons, balloons, stickers, and anything else you think of.

Do something special together. Make birthdays an annual date to share some memories: visit a planetarium, science center, or children's museum; attend a symphonic concert or athletic event; spend time together at the park; go on a canoe, boat, or train ride. Gear the activity to your grandchild's age from year to year.

Birthday book. If you are an avid reader, perhaps you will enjoy sharing your love for books with your grandchild in the form of a collectible "birthday book" each year. Make the book an "in-addition" gift: offer the book in addition to a present your grandchild asks for as an expression of your desire to introduce your grandchild to classic children's literature.

Balloon bouquet in a tree. Fill a small tree in the front yard with balloons that you buy and inflate yourself. Your grandchild will be excited to find his birthday announcement upon coming home from school.

YOUR GIFT-WRAPPING CENTER

Have you ever received a gift wrapped in a handmade, one-of-a-kind package made specially for you? If you have, you know that your appreciation for the giver's thoughtfulness—and sense of anticipation before unwrapping the item—multiplied instantly. Why not take a similar approach to gift-giving with your grandchildren by designing your packages to fit their ages, personalities, and favorite interests? Adding fun little treasures to each gift affirms each child's uniqueness with a caring touch they won't forget.

Store-bought basics to keep on hand:

Gift wrap, tissue, commercially shredded paper and metallics, and gift bags

Ribbon, string, paper and metallic cording, and raffia

Marking pens in various colors and sizes; watercolor paints; rubber stamps and inking kits; colored pencils; stickers

All-purpose glue; fabric glue (spray); paper cement or glue stick; invisible, two-sided, and mailing tape

Glitter and metallic confetti

Mailing labels; small postage scale and a variety of stamps (especially postcard, second ounce, and a few priority) to expedite mailing, if desired

GRANDMA'S COLLECTIBLES

Garage sales, flea markets, craft and hobby stores, estate auctions, and sewing centers are excellent sources of the types of odds-and-ends that make gift packages unique. By picking up things here and there, then storing the items for later, you will soon fill a large storage container with the kind of creative add-ons and bric-a-brac that will make your wraps truly one-of-a-kind.

Wallpaper, felt (great for cutting and gluing into various shapes), fabric scraps, and gift wrap odds-and-ends

Lace, braid, trims, and tassels

Tidbit box: buttons, sequins, beads, and old, inexpensive jewelry

Bright-colored stuffing materials (use as an alternative to commercial tissue): flannel, gingham, calico-prints, netting, and muslin

Nature's artifacts (nonpoisonous only): dried herbs and flowers, twigs, leaves, seed pods, rocks, seashells, feathers, pinecones, decorative grasses, and stardust

Newspapers—especially cartoons and Sunday comic sections

Hankies, bandannas, scarves, pretty napkins, and doilies

Used postcards, sports cards, and greeting cards

Pictures and pages from old books; used sheet music
Pasta in all kinds of shapes
Interesting packages: hang on to any unique promotional or gift bag
Boxes, Styrofoam packing material, and padded mailing envelopes: recycle—buy new only as needed
Stickers, stars, glitter, rubber stamps, assorted ink pads, colored pencils, and metallic pens

Wake-up calls, faxes, and voice mail messages. Whether you can be there in person or not, start out the day with a wake-up by fax or phone, including a special "I love you" message.

Birthday letter. Write a letter to your grandchild in celebration of his life each year, whether she is old enough to read the letter or not. You may want to save these until she is older, to be read all at once, or you can enclose the letter in the birthday card for his mom to read and/or save.

Special song. Does your grandchild have a favorite song? Find out what it is (or choose one that fits), then sing or play it every year after "Happy Birthday."

Collage card. Clip out cartoons, pictures, photos—or whatever else looks interesting—and make a homemade birthday card with hand-written greetings and one-of-a-kind decorations.

Create a "Happy Birthday" poster. Write messages, attach photos, and list your grandchild's "favorites" on a poster board sheet; tack to the entryway or dining room wall.

Birthday events box. When your grandchild is born, create a cultural "time capsule":

1. Place headlines, events, fashion ads, people in the news, food prices, recipes, weather reports, and "what's popular" reviews from newspapers and magazines dated on or near his birthday (or buy a complete newspaper and a set of current magazines (TV, Christian, sports, women's, car, home decorating, literary, computer, etc.) in a large resealable bag.

2. Add a set of present postage stamps and freshly minted collector's coins inside a special collector's tin or decorative box.

134

3. When your grandchild is old enough, get the box out each year and go through it together.

4. If you live far away, make two sets of birthday memorabilia. Keep one complete set at your house for his twenty-first birthday, send the other by mail every year. (Children have a way of losing things!)

Special food. Prepare a meal, or dessert, using your grandchild's favorite recipes. This is an easy way to start a much-appreciated tradition that your kids' kids will look forward to participating in every year. If you live too far away to do this in person, make the treat(s) in advance and send the birthday package by express or priority mail.

Memory book. At the birthday party, ask each person to write his or her favorite memory of the child, from the current year, in a memory book. Repeat again next year (and the year after and . . .) Later, you may add photos from the year, several birthday cards, descriptions of humorous events, guest list, audio or videotape recording of guests' "live interviews", etc.

"It's Your Day" tablecloth or placemat. Buy a twin-size sheet; decorate it with your grandchild's name, using permanent markers. Provide a laundry-proof marking pen for guests every year and have them autograph it. Use the tablecloth every year, adding new comments on each occasion. Or, create a one-of-a-kind placemat. Make a fabric or paper placemat; ask family members to add their handwritten, humorous observations, recognition of accomplishments, commendations for good behavior, and loving affirmations, including special encouragement for the year ahead. The placemat may be laminated and stored with your grandchild's memory book.

> *What an enormous magnifier is tradition! How a thing grows in the human memory and in the human imagination, when love, worship, and all that lies in the human heart, is there to encourage it.*
> Thomas Carlyle

Surprise party in a package. If you live too far away to attend your grandchild's birthday and you know that tight finances will make it difficult for your child to host a party, sponsor one for him. Pack up a large mailing box with everything your grandchild will need: decorations, plates, napkins, hats, favors, candles, cake and frosting mix, presents, a few simple games, and a disposable camera for Mom to take pictures. Include a postpaid mailer so the camera and film may be returned to you for film developing.

Birthday blessing. Write, sing, or share a "birthday blessing" with your grandchild using a Bible verse, hand-printed psalm, or other faith expression that celebrates your grandchild's Christian heritage.

Annual candle. Use an "anniversary" candle or make your own: light the candle at the beginning of the celebration, then burn the candle until it touches the next year's mark.

Birthday circle. Sit in a circle with the birthday person in the center. Ask each family member to share something he or she enjoys, appreciates, or cherishes about the person, then have someone say a prayer for him. You may also want to have the person open gifts before or after your family's sharing time.

Lighting the birthday cake. Have each person put a candle on the cake, saying something he or she appreciates about the birthday guest. For added dramatic effect, turn off the lights before lighting the candles. If there is a special song your grandchild enjoys, sing it in addition to "Happy Birthday."

Give your grandchild a "birthday plate." Buy a keepsake plate and have it personalized with your grandchild's name. Fill the plate with homemade goodies, asking your grandchild to return the plate to you after the treats are finished; repeat every year. When your grandkids become grandparents, who knows? Perhaps they will carry on this lovely annual tradition with their grandchildren.

Family Reunions

In spite of all the years that have passed, reunions remind us that family relationships continue—a firmly rooted part of our identity. Something special happens when we make it a priority to be with family members, away from home and work responsibilities, for an extended weekend—or even an entire week. We can grow closer together and gain greater insight into our parents, siblings (and, if they're around, our cousins, nieces, nephews, aunts, uncles, and grandparents), and ourselves. We create new traditions and celebrate old ones. We reconnect with our past. We think about where our family will be heading in the future.

Once grandchildren arrive, nieces, nephews, and cousins also multiply—another good reason to plan regular family get-togethers. Giving the next generation an opportunity to meet and get to know each other is vitally important, a time when family stories, pictures, jokes, memories, songs, and videos can be enjoyed by your collective clan.

POSSIBLE REUNION SITES

- State park or national campground
- Resort area condominium or motel
- "Residential suite" hotel
- Family-oriented bed-and-breakfast (reserve entire house)
- Lakeside lodge or cabin
- Sightseeing center: coastal California, Grand Canyon, Washington D.C., Great Lakes, country music (Nashville, TN or Branson, MO), Disney World, etc.
- Caribbean cruise ship or all-inclusive Mexican beach hotel package
- Clubhouse, retreat center, or community hall
- Your home

As you plan your gathering, consider ways to get everyone involved in organizing the reunion. Take it step-by-step. To increase the likelihood of your family's full participation, include your children at each stage in the process.

Express your enthusiasm. Decide how you would like to approach the reunion. Make phone calls—or better yet, send out a letter—to invite everyone's participation in organizing the reunion and setting its goals.

Make a short list of possible locations. Research possible sites and estimated expenses, make a short list of your suggestions, then find out your children's preferences. Offer at least four locations, listing approximate costs, along with four or five possible dates: the Fourth of July, first weekend in August, Thanksgiving, and Christmas, for example. Include the specific location of each suggested site in your letter with proposed activities and meal ideas (potluck, eating out, home-cooked, catered, or your own custom blend). Ask everyone to rank their preferences by number. Some popular reunion locations are listed in the sidebar on page 137.

Do not—I repeat, do not—expect everyone to come. No matter how well you plan, it's going to be extremely difficult to find a time, date, and location that will fit everyone's schedule and individual family budget. Go ahead and meet with those who can come. If you can afford it, offer to pay the cost of everyone's travel and/or room expenses.

Delegate reunion-related responsibilities. In a follow-up letter, share your excitement about the upcoming reunion. Decide who will be the reunion's coordinator—it may be you or someone else. The coordinator will be the one to keep everyone up-to-date and enthusiastic about the event. Send out a sign-up sheet listing the areas and responsibilities the coordinator will need help with:

—meals: plan menus, buy food and supplies, oversee meal preparation

—lodging: research possible sites and accommodations, make reservations, supervise check-in and check-out

—money: estimate expenses, collect funds, make deposits, pay bills

—phoning and mailing: set up a "clearing" center, write and copy letters, make follow-up calls, collect five to ten dollars from each family to cover communication costs

—custodial: set up and tear down bedding, coordinate bath, kitchen, and living area cleanup, supervise waste disposal

Consider all age groups represented at the reunion. Plan children's activities to support their preference for interacting with same-age family members: playtime for toddlers; easy projects for preschoolers; hikes, sports, and outings for elementary-age children; and teen activities away from the adults (with supervision, if needed). Scheduling several all-inclusive family times that include every age group—such as a campfire, Sunday morning service, talent festival, photo-op session, baseball or volleyball game, Music Night, story-telling sessions, world-premiere home video screening, funny field games—will prove especially memorable.

After the reunion, put together memory books or small photo albums of your time together. Make copies of your favorite pictures and personal comments; mail the finished result with a "WE DID IT!" declaration enclosed. Later, if everyone seems interested in having another reunion, why not make it an annual or semiannual tradition?

The Family Table

Good things happen when we sit down at the table and break bread together. In these days of fast food and hectic schedules, it's more important than ever for families to reclaim the special joys of eating together. For example, you can:

Invite your children and grandchildren over for breakfast occasionally. Breakfast is a fun way to share a family meal on the weekend. Waffles, made-to-order omelettes, huevos rancheros, or fruit-filled pancakes will say "Good Morning" to everyone with a home-cooked meal that tends to be easier and faster than making a complete dinner for everybody. And afterward, the rest of your day is left open for other activities.

Hold seasonal progressive dinners. Why view progressive dinners as a church-related activity only? If you live near your children, suggest a progressive dinner with as many courses as your homes will allow. Another advantage to this plan: progressive dinners can be easily arranged to accommodate different dining area sizes, with appetizer, soup and salad, and/or dessert courses planned for the smallest spaces. Ask everyone to bring copies of their recipes for sharing.

Let them eat cake—or pie. Sometimes, it's nice to separate dessert from regular meals and special parties by making it a course of its own. It's no longer necessary to feel guilt-ridden when eating dessert, either— many great-tasting recipes, as you already know, now incorporate low-fat alternatives to traditional, high-calorie fare. Ask everyone to bring a dessert from the same category to share; slice or scoop in small portions on a sampler plate. Serve with delicious fresh-brewed tea or coffee. And don't forget to exchange recipes!

Share the load. Potluck (or "pot blessing," if you prefer) family meals allow family members to share the cooking responsibilities when you are too busy to shop, fix, and serve an entire meal, and yet still promotes family sharing around the table.

Have an "International Night" supper. International cooking is an educational experience, ranging from meal planning research at the library, shopping in ethnic food stores, preparing foreign foods, and designing a fitting presentation. And it's a nice way to incorporate missions-mindedness into a family celebration, and provides yet another opportunity for recipe sharing. Pick an ethnic or regional theme—Greek, Italian, Ethiopian, Peruvian, or Thai, for instance—and see how much fun young and old alike can have in getting involved with the dinner. Make this meal a potluck adventure, if you like. If it's a success, consider turning your "International Night" into a seasonal celebration.

Entertain your grandchildren during meal preparation. Use white paper for a tablecloth, and give your grandchildren crayons, markers, or colored pencils to draw "centerpiece" pictures as their contribution to the table decorations.

Celebrate the end (or beginning, or middle) of summer with an ice cream social. Homemade ice cream or frozen yogurt is a special treat for kids of all ages. Plan a simple meal, with paper plates for easy clean-up, and then spend time after dinner making the dessert together. Prepare a variety of toppings in advance: try fresh fruit and edible flowers (violets, nasturtiums, daylilies, roses, or lavender) for a pleasant change of pace.

Hold a cook-off. Hold a backyard barbecue, baking extravaganza, chili competition, best chocolate chip cookie, or pizza-making contest are just a few of the fun possibilities for your family's consideration and invited participation.

Sample fondue. Using a fondue pot or crockery cooker, experiment with a variety of tasty recipes. Fruit, vegetables, cheese, angel food cake, and chopped meats are just a few of the dipping delights to try with different sauces. Sample one at a time as part of a simple meal or offer as a dessert or snack. The appeal of these delectable treats comes from the congenial atmosphere created as you sit together around the goodies, talking and taking turns.

Publish a family cookbook. Homemade family cookbooks are among the best cookbooks in America today. If your family is interested, include your grandchildren in helping you publish one. Here is how to publish a collection of your family's favorite recipes—with your grandchildren's expert assistance, of course.

1. Conduct a recipe swap, asking everyone to send in their favorite recipes, including source, anecdotes associated with the recipe, and informal taste-test results.

2. Sort the recipes, by family or food category (appetizers and beverages, soups and salads, breads, etc.), and type them out or enter them on your personal computer. Decorate the pages and handwrite the recipe names, if you like.

3. Take the resulting book to your local printer, where the book can be copied and spiral bound for about six or seven dollars each.

4. Give the books to your children or, if your finances are tight, ask them to help you cover copying and mailing costs.

Giving Gifts They'll Enjoy and Appreciate

Receiving a specially selected gift with a handmade card from a grandparent is meaningful to young children. It's not that they don't appreciate receiving commercially made cards with checks enclosed. They do. But unwrapping a surprise that suits one's personal interests and identity is better.

If you are not certain about what gift to choose, ask one of your grandchild's parents. In addition, I have included some early suggestions below for your consideration.

> *Amazing things begin to happen when we enter the world of the child. Both the child and the adult are enriched.*
> Dr. Paul Welter,
> *Learning from Children*

Treats for Babies and Toddlers

Baby's bath bag. Arrange animal-shaped glycerin soaps and sponges, bath toys, baby shampoo, brightly printed washcloths and a towel in a plastic, and preferably drainable, bag with a handle that can be conveniently kept in the linen closet or under the sink.

"From Grandma's (or Grandpa's) Bookshelf" crate. Begin with specially designed-for-infants fabric, vinyl, and heavy board books. As your grandchild grows, you can regularly add to the collection, first given in a wooden or plastic crate, with age-appropriate contributions—Bible stories, delightful picture books, bright-colored easy readers, etc.

Beach pail. Fill a brand-new covered plastic garbage pail with a rolled up hat, sunglasses, baby (or children's) sunscreen lotion, plastic ball and water toys, beach towel, sifter, and shovel.

Bedtime treasure chest. Tie lace or bright-colored fabric ribbon on a wicker basket containing a night-light, lullaby cassette tape, bedtime book, teddy bear, and blanket.

Putting-things-together basket. Load a bright-colored plastic laundry basket with plastic measuring cups and a variety of dexterity toys that encourage your grandchild to pull, push, press, twist, turn, take apart, sort, stack, mix, and match things.

Budding artist's sack. Give your toddler-age grandchild a plastic apron, pad of paper, selection of children's brushes, box of crayons, and a set of red, yellow, and blue non-toxic children's paint tucked in a decorated carrying bag.

Preschoolers' Gift Boxes

Tool kit. Assemble a batch of children's tools. Place them in a real tool box with a few "adult" items, such as a plastic ruler, cloth or plastic measuring tape; washable, non-toxic colored markers, sponge-tipped paintbrush, pieces of wood, small "worker's" apron, washable school glue, and a pint of washable, non-toxic children's paint. Add more supplies to the box as your grandchild grows, supplying "real" items to replace imitations.

Art box. Purchase a plastic artist's box from a discount craft store. Load the box with colored chalk, pens, pencils, erasers, brushes, watercolor paint, stickers, school glue, non-toxic paste, and safety scissors. Tie a big ribbon around the box, a children's art book, and several pads of paper in various sizes.

Wardrobe closet. Buy a cardboard wardrobe box from a moving company or discount store. Create a dress-up wardrobe for your granddaughter from garage sales, thrift shops, and your own closet: shoes, ribbons, socks, slips, silk flower hairpieces, skirts, blouses, barrettes, scarves, fancy dresses, and hats of all kinds. Wrap the contents in multiple layers of pretty tissue with a floral-scented sachet tucked inside.

Builder's dream. If your grandchild likes to put things together, buy several different types of small building kits—Lego, Brio, wooden blocks, Lincoln Logs—and put them, wrapped, in a big box (also wrapped).

Grocery store stock. Save those containers, grandparents! Kids love playing "grocery store" with clean, used paper and plastic cartons: cocoa, oatmeal, breakfast cereal, sugar cubes, spices, baking soda, instant pudding, converted rice, sour cream, refrigerated orange juice, taco shells, eggs, cake mixes, and raisins are all packaged in reusable, unbreakable packages. When you're finished collecting store items, wrap them in a large box with a bright-colored bow on top.

Doll trunk. If a baby doll is your gift choice, wrap the life-sized doll in a special trunk along with an assortment of real baby items: a dress or short suit, nightgown, sweater, bonnet, kimono set, booties, and bib, bought at thrift stores or garage sales, then cleaned and pressed. Place a soft blanket, baby rattle, teething ring, and a small package of newborn-size disposable diapers in a separate, wrapped box.

Collector's cabinet. Pack a covered plastic container with items related to your grandchild's hobby. For example, if your grandchild is interested in sports, save sports magazines, game programs, team schedules, newspaper pictures and articles to include in the box; add several packs of sports cards, a favorite team's T-shirt and cap, storage boxes, and a tube-protected sports poster.

Celebrating All Year Long

There's always a reason to celebrate! In this section you'll find both time-tested holiday traditions and new ideas you may want to try.

Valentine's Day

Commemorate Valentine's as "Celebrate Love" Day. Fill a special jar or a box with Bible verses about love and "love notes" to your grandchild, written on brightly colored construction paper.

Read a special story. Buy your grandchild a book about love; read it together—or send the book with your read-aloud cassette tape.

Make hand-made valentines. These can be simple—made with construction paper, glitter, glue, stickers, and colored pens—or fabulously ornate—fabric cards with embroidery, lace, antique buttons, and appliqué; cookie valentines (hand-decorated sugar, honey, or molasses heart-shaped cookies or gingerbread people painted to look like family members); or heirloom valentines arranged in a special shadow box collection with your signed message on the back.

Go out for dessert. Take your grandchild to his or her favorite dessert spot and swap Valentines.

Affirm your affection. Valentine's Day is a good time to say "I love you," in person or by phone, by blessing your grandchild with an affirming message he doesn't have to earn.

Make a festive meal. Use your imagination to create homemade treats: heart-shaped bread, a cherry or raspberry gelatin mold, gingerbread with confectioners' sugar sprinkled through a heart-shaped paper doily, chocolate cupcakes covered with red-colored toppings.

St. Patrick's Day

Talk about family history. If your family's ancestors were Irish, it's a great time to pass along what you know about your background, including the history of St. Patrick. Make a tape recording, read a story, send a letter. Whether in person or from a distance, teach something new to your grandchild about his heritage each year.

Share Ireland's unique Christian heritage. Read about Ireland's famous saints—including Brigid, Fiacre, Columba, and, of course, Patrick; tell your grandchildren about how Christianity came to the Emerald Isle.

Go for the green. Wear it, color your food and beverages with it, deck the walls in it.

Make a traditional Irish meal. Even if you're not Irish, St. Patrick's Day can be fun. Invite the family over for some soda bread, corned beef, and cabbage. For added entertainment, play Celtic hymns on your stereo system while quizzing guests, asking five or ten questions about Ireland (Why is Ireland called the "Emerald Isle"? Why is St. Patrick Ireland's patron saint? Who was St. Columba?).

Read an Irish story. Is one of your favorite children's stories set in Ireland? Share it with your grandchild—in person, over the phone, or by mail.

Resurrection Sunday (Easter)

Remember Resurrection morning together. Sunrise services, special devotions, and hot cross buns are part of many families' Resurrection Day celebration. Will they be part of yours, too?

Make Easter baskets with a Christian theme. Replace most, or all, candy with Bible storybooks, kids' praise tapes, and a handmade card celebrating Jesus' resurrection.

Hold a family sunrise service. Ask each family member to contribute something: a Scripture passage, song, psalm, poem, or personal reflections about Jesus' triumph. Welcome everyone into the kitchen for a made-in-advance Easter morning meal of hot cross buns, fruit salad, ham-and-egg casserole, and juice. Weather permitting, go for a walk together after breakfast.

Share traditional Easter symbols with a distinctly Christian message.

—Egg coloring. Create your own natural egg-dyes and decorations. Before dyeing, decorate eggshells with uniquely-yours Christian motifs, using a needle or wax marker. Place one dozen eggs in a large pan with two cups natural pigment materials—coffee, cherries, blueberries, spinach, red cabbage, raw shredded beets, or five to six pieces saffron—then cover with water, add one tablespoon vinegar, and simmer for fifteen minutes. Turn off stove and leave eggs covered for one hour; dry on paper towels. Brush with vegetable oil.

—Egg hunt. Fill plastic eggs with Bible verses, "love coupons" (something special the parents and grandparents will do with or for the child), and small surprises. After hiding the eggs around the yard, have your grandchildren find them. Gather together afterward and tell or read them the story of Resurrection morning. Give each child a remembrance of the event: an angel pin, a small Bible storybook, etc.

—Easter basket. Decorate a box with bright-colored wrapping paper, foil, tissue, or construction paper; fill with green paper strips (tissue or construction paper) and things to remember Jesus by—a children's Bible, cassette tape of children's praise songs, cross, and Nativity scene.

Cook a traditional Easter dinner. Why not serve your signature dish—honey-glazed ham, scalloped potato kugel, or roast lamb—every year? When they're old enough, the children can help you decorate the dining area with things that remind them of Easter. And don't forget the daffodils.

Mother's Day

Help your grandchild prepare Mom's gift. With assistance, your grandchild can become a published author, accomplished artist, or celebrated cook. Would his mom enjoy a hand-made book, framed

> *Let the children laugh and be glad . . . .*
> *Laugh with them, till tears run down your faces—*
> *till a memory of pure delight and precious*
> *relationship is established within them,*
> *indestructible, personal, and forever.*
> Walter Wangerin,
> *Ragman and Other Cries of Faith*

picture, or homemade brownies? Invite him to your house before Mother's Day for the purpose of helping him create a one-of-a-kind treasure.

Honor your daughter as the mother of your grandchild. Mother's Day is for moms, even if they do happen to be our daughters. Mothers of still-at-home children have few personal advocates. It's a demanding job, remember? Now that we're older, with grown children, we can turn our attention to supporting our successors.

Give your daughter something special. Find a gift you won't have to buy—an heirloom, a framed, antique family picture (copied professionally), her baby book—that conveys how much you cherish your daughter. She'll appreciate being affirmed in her maternal role by you—her mother. Or, if she doesn't have one yet, get your daughter a coffeemaker, answering machine, or cordless phone.

Celebrate the gift of life. Make a donation in your daughter's name to an adoption agency, children's mission fund, or crisis pregnancy center; send a beautiful card thanking her for opening up her heart to motherhood.

Father's Day

Commemorate your son's fatherhood. The same thoughts and ideas I've shared for Mother's Day apply here: once your grandchild arrives, Father's Day becomes your son's day, too. It's an excellent time for a clan gathering, with all three generations represented, as you celebrate each father's family contributions.

Encourage his playfulness. No matter how old your son gets, he will probably always enjoy receiving gifts he can experiment or tinker with: a model airplane, rock-tumbling kit, kites. And now that he's a dad, he can include his family in the fun.

More ideas for gifts that he'll appreciate. Here are some ideas (gleaned from my own family and friends) that were big hits as Father's Day presents: a Duncan yo-yo; tickets to a professional baseball game; new tools; a brand-new bicycle and helmet; a Horner harmonica; professional car cleaning ("The Works"); recent novel by a favorite author wrapped up in a new hammock; a collectible sports card and the latest copy of *Beckett* magazine; a fullyloaded Swiss Army knife.

Grandparents' Day

Forget the cards, the flowers, and the presents. Grandparents' Day was first observed in 1978 by a group of Midwestern grandparents who simply wanted to say: Grandparents are worth celebrating, too. We can mark the moment annually by demonstrating how much we care about our grandchildren on "our" day. What Grandparents' Day is really all about is commemorating the unique role we play in our family's lives. Make your day count.

Reaffirm family connections. Either in person or on the phone, set time aside on Grandparents' Day to tell your grandchildren how much you love and appreciate them. If possible, do something together.

Share your skills. Use your day as an opportunity to show your children and grandchildren how your grandparenting skills enrich their lives: storytelling, a family meal, going to an unusual and fun place you'd like to tell them about.

Reflect on your role. Is there anything you would prefer to do differently in relation to grandparenting? What are your goals as a grandparent for the coming year? Are you especially pleased or dissatisfied about a particular aspect of grandparenting? Would you like to strengthen your bond with your grandchild in the next few months? How will you do this?

Honor your identity. Give yourself a pat on the back—you are a grandparent, and that is a fact worth celebrating. You are a very important person in your grandchild's life. Take joy in appreciating the wonder of your relationship.

All Saints' Day

Observe the Christian holiday after Halloween is over. Leave the witches and the goblins behind and rediscover what all the pagans were ranting about: a feast celebration of the martyrs and saints who loved and served the Lord.

Hold a treasure hunt. Hide small "surprise packs" around the house that contain one or two items (colored markers, crayons, coloring books, packages of Play-Doh, Bible storybooks, etc.), with a total of three to five packs per grandchild. Create a treasure map, listing a separate clue for each "treasure" on the child's individual route.

Invite your grandchildren over for a "feast day." Buy an illustrated book with short stories about famous saints. Talk about early church traditions and a few saints' lives before or after dinner. Make the dinner special, including a blessing on the food in remembrance of the heroes of our faith, by using candles and china and a centerpiece of fresh flowers.

Play Bible games. Check your local Christian bookstore for books and products that will help you make the evening fun as well as memorable.

Thanksgiving

Prepare a thank-you basket. Place small notecards or paper scraps near a basket with several pens. As guests arrive, ask them to write down something they are especially thankful for right now, then place the paper in a basket to be shared before (or after) dinner.

Invite your grandchildren over to watch televised parades. By the time the Thanksgiving parades start, you will be ready to take a break from cooking. Serve an easy brunch buffet—fruit juice, bagels, yogurt, and muffins—to be taken on trays to your in-house viewing stands. And if it's early enough, ask the kids to come in their pajamas.

Recruit the local art talent. Buy a piece of paper to fit your front door. Assemble a collection of markers and crayons. Invite guests of all ages to draw someone or something from the first Thanksgiving: Native Americans, pilgrims, cornstalks, pumpkins. Tape on the front door when finished.

Start a new tradition. If your children's in-laws feel more strongly about getting together on Thanksgiving than you do, hold your feast on Friday or Saturday. Children are off school for the entire weekend, as are most parents.

Include everyone in fixing the meal. Dividing up the tasks according to age and ability, assign each person a part of the meal. You will be surprised how capable a closely supervised three-year-old can be.

Participate in a round-the-table blessing. Invite each person to offer God thanks individually before passing the food, saying that those who are shy about praying aloud may remain silent. If you are worried about the food getting cold, wait until the blessing is over before bringing out certain items, or use electric warmers.

Delegate cleanup duties. Write down various each job to be done on a small piece of paper. Possibilities include: mashing potatoes, making gravy, sweeping the floor, folding napkins, pouring beverages, lighting candles, decorating the table, squirting whipped topping on the pie, loading the dishwasher, and wrapping up leftovers. When finished, divide the pieces into two piles: one for older children and adults, the other for the younger ones. Place each pile in a separate covered container, shake, and distribute evenly. Later, play funny music (John Philip Sousa marches or Broadway show tunes work great) during the cleanup and don't dump the turkey grease down the kitchen sink—plumbers' profits soar during the week after Thanksgiving due to emergency calls aimed at unclogging drainage pipes. Use paper plates for dessert—to be served when the table is cleared and the dishes loaded or washed.

Watch a movie together on the VCR. If you want to see a video on Thanksgiving evening, *It's a Wonderful Life* is a best bet. *Heidi* is another good choice.

Advent (The Four Sundays before Christmas)

Send your grandchildren their own Advent calendars. Shop early for the best selection, choosing from a wide variety of colorful cards, wall decorations, and reusable wooden advent calendars. Or, you may make your own from scratch—needlecraft kits and seasonal books offer numerous ideas.

Ask your grandchildren to help you decorate. Invite your grandchild over for a treetrimming party. If your grandchild is young, provide ornaments that will not break, assigning him a "just-for-you," easily accessible area of the tree. Play and sing Christmas carols during the festivities or afterward, when you darken the room, turn on the tree lights, and relax together on the sofa or floor with a cup of cider or hot chocolate.

Celebrate the Sundays of Advent with a late afternoon or an early evening service. If you wish, use an Advent wreath and candles: light one new candle every week for four weeks, with the fifth candle lighted on Christmas Day. Progressively read portions of the Gospel of St. Matthew, pray together, sing carols and worship songs. Serve dinner or a dessert afterward.

Create homemade ornaments for your grandchildren. Clothespin tin soldiers, felt dolls, gingerbread people, crocheted snowflakes, tinfoil stars, bread-dough Santas . . . potential creative ideas abound. And if you make this an annual tradition, your grandchildren will have a great collection to take along when they have homes of their own.

Take them to see a live ballet production of The Nutcracker. If your community offers a live ballet performance of *The Nutcracker Suite*, take your grandchild as soon as he is old enough to enjoy it (and sit quietly while doing so), or rent the American Ballet Theater's taped version and watch it together on television.

Hold a cookie-baking party. Round up the aprons and cookie sheets. Forget about flour spills and sticky counters. Cooking, baking—and gingerbread-house making—are delightful ways to celebrate the season with grandchildren. Prepare refrigerator dough ahead of time if you prefer, focusing on rolling, cutting, and decorating only. Give your grandchild an ample selection to take home, with an illustrated book of the Christmas story tucked inside the cookie bag.

Christmas

Make a traditional Christmas Eve buffet dinner. Use historic family recipes or introduce new ones of your own, if needed. Consider your ethnic background when sorting through possible choices. Spend extra time planning, making, and arranging the banquet table decorations; ask older grandchildren for assistance.

Attend a Christmas Eve worship service. Candles, carols, and communion make the night one of the most memorable Christian celebrations of the year. Your grandchild will enjoy being included in this jubilant holiday tradition.

Light luminaria candles on Christmas Eve. A favorite tradition of many families is to line the front walkway with decorative paper bags, weighted with sand and lighted by votive candles, sometime after sundown on Christmas Eve. You may also want to turn off the lights in the main part of your house and sing carols by candlelight—a wonderful follow-up to the evening's eggnog and buffet dinner.

Bake a "Happy Birthday, Jesus!" cake. Make a Santa Lucia ring (a Scandinavian coffee cake decorated with confectioner's sugar icing, cherries, and candles) or a regular birthday cake to commemorate baby Jesus' birth for your grandchildren.

Start a new gift-giving tradition. If you want to exchange your past approach to gift-giving for a new tradition this year, consider trying one of these tried-and-true family favorites:

—Draw names. Once your family grows too big to easily exchange gifts, or lives too far apart to send packages inexpensively, agree on a name-drawing method and dollar amount everyone feels comfortable with, asking for a fair-minded volunteer to oversee the process.

—Give handmade items. Did you know that a famous Hollywood actress now insists on exchanging only handmade gifts with her superstar husband? The turning point came when he gave her a twenty-carat diamond ring, provoking her to reconsider their escalating expectations. Not a bad idea—in fact, this is one new/old tradition I think we'll be trying out as a family this year.

—Donate gifts and/or time to charity. Invite your family or grandchildren to participate with you in expressing Christ's love for the poor. Christian organizations in your community offer a wide variety of opportunities. Read Dickens' *A Christmas Carol* to your grandchildren to emphasize the importance of giving.

—Rotate the "big gift." Some parents rotate the adult child they give a large gift ($100 and up) to every year—a piece of furniture, needed appliance, etc. This way, gift-giving doesn't deplete the bank account, and substantial gifts are distributed equally over the years. It also leaves more money for the grandchildren.

Create a St. Nicholas corner in your home. If space allows, close off a room, closet, or workspace where you can set up all of your gifts and wrapping supplies. Trim the door with a "Santa's Workshop—Do Not Open Until December 25" sign and other fun decorations to increase your grandchildren's sense of anticipation.

New Year's Eve & Day

Hold a "watch night" supper and midnight service. Welcome the new year in with a late-night pizza or potluck appetizer buffet, hot mulled cider, and cranberry punch. Follow the meal with a praise chorus and hymn sing-along; review the highlights of your year as you "watch" for the new one's arrival. Shortly before midnight, spend time in prayerful reflection and worship together.

Have a family pajama party. Why go out on a night that's notorious for drunken driving when you can stay at home in your robe and pajamas? Have the family bring their sleeping bags for late-night storytelling and reminiscing.

Celebrate with your family's favorite games. Invite everyone over for an afternoon game marathon using time-tested favorites. Serve luncheon leftovers during one of the football games later in the day.

Cook a wonderful breakfast everyone will think about until next year. Check out *The Breakfast Book* by Marion Cunningham, the editor of the *Fannie Farmer Cookbook,* for possible recipes. It's filled with great ideas (including an etiquette chart!) and menus for making your New Year's breakfasts truly remarkable.

Meet for lunch at a nearby restaurant. Tired of holiday cooking? Treat the family to a midmorning brunch or late lunch. Let someone else do the work while you relax and have fun together.

Make New Year's Day the time you take down the tree and put away Christmas decorations. If your fresh-cut tree can make it through to New Year's Day, establish a tradition of Christmas decoration take-down on New Year's Day, followed by a festive snack or dessert.

Vacationing and Traveling Together

If you're traveling as an extended family, naturally the primary responsibility for meeting your grandchild's needs will belong to your daughter and son-in-law. You'll be a much-welcomed source of diversion, helping to keep that small traveler occupied and happy! If you're on your own with your grandchild, however, there'll be lots more to think about. Survey the tips that follow, picking and choosing to fit your circumstances.

Making Travel Easier (and Safer)

Don't forget the car seat. For a free, up-to-date pamphlet on choosing a safe car seat, "Family Shopping Guide to Car Seats," write to the American Academy of Pediatrics, P.O. Box 927, Elk Grove Village, IL 60009-0927. An updated list of car seat recalls and a shopper's guide is available by phone from the National Highway Traffic Safety Administration's toll-free, twenty four hour hotline as well. Call (800) 424-9393 to request this information (or 366-0123, if you live in the Washington, D.C. area).

Get ready for longer trips. For just fifty cents, you can obtain "Merrily We Roll Along," a brochure that will tell you creative ways to help keep your grandchild happy during car travel. Request it from the National Association for the Education for Young Children (NAEYC), 1509 Sixteenth Street, N.W., Washington, D.C. 20036-1426; (800) 424-2460.

Provide travel toys. Here are a few suggestions, to be wrapped ahead of time as a surprise to open on the trip.

—Busy Baby car seat toys. Four colorful infant and toddler toys, attached to twenty colorful plastic links, will keep your grandchild busy

Easing Baby Car Travel

- Music. Play tapes or sing songs that will soothe your grandchild when fussy, interest him when bored, and help you to unwind when your stress level builds.
- Tidying up. For quick cleanups, store wet wipes and paper towels within easy reach; place a thick towel or plastic tablecloth under the car seat to spare upholstery from spills.
- Soft toys. Tie a variety of toys to the baby's seat to keep them from getting lost—or thrown across the car.
- Dressing right for the occasion. As heating or air conditioning changes the temperature inside the car, remember to appropriately adjust your grandchild's clothing by unwrapping his blankets, removing extra garments, or covering exposed skin with a lightweight baby afghan.
- Photo play. Attach a colorful picture in front of the baby on the back of the passenger seat when he's facing the rear of the car.
- Sun shades. Reduce eye discomfort from sun glare by securing a transparent shade to any window affecting your grandchild.
- Keeping cool. During warm months, drape the baby's car seat with a big white towel to deflect heat whenever your car is parked in the sun.
- Dining out. Try to time your meals when restaurant business is slow (usually 9–11AM, 2–5PM, and 8–11PM, excluding Sunday). Ask for a table in the non-smoking section by a window where your grandchild can stay busy watching people and cars go by; if he's sleeping, request a quiet spot away from the kitchen and rest rooms.

as you drive. Available from Toys to Grow On, (800) 874-4242. Nested plastic measuring cups and measuring spoons are fun, too.

—Grandma's purse. Fill an old purse with age-appropriate items. For a baby, plastic keys, a fun mirror, soft and squishy animals, and a multitextured ball work well; a toddler will enjoy things he can touch, put together, and pull apart; preschoolers like imitations of grown-up stuff, such as playing cards, plastic-protected purse mirror, and a magnifying glass.

—Books about transportation. Give your grandchild several books, geared to his age group, showing bright-colored pictures of cars, boats, trains, and planes.

—Travel Ghost Writer. Made by the Ohio Art company, the

makers of Etch-a-Sketch, this smaller version Ghost Writer features a wide pen and an erasable drawing board—shake it, and the picture disappears. It's available at most toy stores.

—Music box. Pack a small, lid-covered container with things that make music—the kind that you won't mind listening to.

—Travel games. Many older children's games come in travel sizes. Pressman, for example, makes a six-in-one magnetic travel game for playing six perennially popular board games, including chess, checkers, and backgammon. Check your local toy store for what's currently available.

—Art kit. Load a canvas bag with non-toxic art supplies specially designed for your grandchild's age and abilities—pads of different sizes and colors of paper, colored pencils and markers, children's scissors, cut-out activity books, pressure-sensitive dots and stickers, peel-and-stick plastic shapes (stored in a resealable bag), and crayons and coloring books.

Food and beverages. Be sure your grandchild has enough to drink; traveling by car and air dehydrates the body. Freeze a few cartons of juice, allowing for en route defrosting; pack foods that won't spoil— cereal squares, rice cakes, unsalted crackers; ask your grandchild, once he is old enough, to help you pack a snack sack (or insulated, blue-ice chilled lunchbox) with his favorite foods.

Take repeated breaks. Make frequent, once-an-hour stops to allow for exercise, hugs, stretching, and potty breaks. Generously estimate the length of your trip.

Stave off boredom with games. Check out the bibliography in Additional Resources, page 209 for a list of great suggestions.

Prepare for unexpected bad weather and road trouble. Bring a first-aid kit, umbrella, emergency flashlight, and a blanket.

For Those Special Trips
Consider using an agency that specializes in planning grandparent-grandchild trips, or join a travel club. Grandtravel, located in Chevy Chase, Maryland, is a travel agency that coordinates trips in Washing-

ton, D.C., Williamsburg, Virginia, and along the Maine coast. Their phone number is (800) 247-7651. Another travel group, Vistatours, offers trips for grandparents and grandchildren in New England, South Dakota, and Nevada. They can be contacted at (800) 248-4782. Numerous travel clubs—AAA, Citibank, and ITC, for example—offer attractive, lower cost inclusive packages and provide substantial discounts to members for a fee.

Learn about where you're going to visit. Whether your destination lies stateside or in a foreign country, it's a great idea to find out what you can about the place ahead of time. A travel agent can provide you with brochures and tourist information. Check your local bookstore and public library for additional information. In the U.S., call the tourism department of the state you'll be visiting and request a current traveler's packet. For a free copy of "Discover America: A Listing of State and Territorial Travel Offices of the United States," send your request to the Consumer Information Center, P.O. Box 100, Pueblo, Colorado 81002. "Information Please," which provides the phone numbers for Visitors Bureaus in all fifty states, plus the numbers for major hotel chains, airlines, and car rental agencies, is available from the Family Travel Guides Catalogue, P.O. Box 6061, Albany, California 94706-0061; (510) 527-5849.

Read for ideas. Recommended books:

—*The Best Bargain Family Vacations* by Laura Sutherland and Valerie Wolf Deutsch (St. Martin's Press, 1993). Describes over two hundred affordable family vacation destinations in the United States, including camps, dude ranches, parks, and resorts. Travel hints, budget hotel listings, and travel information center numbers are also given.

—*Places to Go with Children* by various authors (Chronicle Books). Travel guide series specifically oriented to family-centered vacation locations and attractions. Each book focuses on a different location.

—*The Family Travel Guide*, edited by Carole Terwilliger Meyers (Carousel Press, 1994). Extensive collection of travel articles and timely tips by different authors about taking trips with children.

Reserve in advance. Airlines, car leasing agents, and hotel chains fill up fast during peak travel seasons. By avoiding last-minute plans, you'll save yourself money, time, and headaches. Find out when the busiest hours are; plan your trip during less busy times. If you reserve a seat for a baby or toddler, you'll be required to bring a car seat—safety-tested for airline travel and equipped with a locking clip for seat belt attachment—that fits into the plane's seat. Tell the airline representative the age of your young flying companion and ask what special services are available, such as children's menus, bottle and baby food warming, preboarding, and airport changing tables. When traveling with a grandchild under five, request a bulkhead seat reservation for extra room.

Plan on additional time for checking in and plane changes during layovers. Bring a collapsible stroller on board—they're allowed—for easier between-flight walking. (Full-size strollers may be "gate-checked" as you board the plane, but won't be available during flight changes.)

11
Leaving a Lasting Legacy

Think of a family treasure you received from a parent or grandparent. The old family photograph or your grandma's recipe box may be every bit as precious to you as something with high monetary value such as an engagement ring or an antique vase.

Like you, your grandchildren will also appreciate having something of Grandma's or Grandpa's to remind them of their unique heritage and of the special person you are in their lives. Your one-of-a-kind gifts will be treasured for many years to come. Though it may take considerable energy, thought, and time to organize what you want to pass on to your grandchildren, the results will be priceless.

Creating Your Family Archives

Wouldn't it be wonderful if all grandparents left a lasting record of their family's history for their grandchildren? Creating such a record involves work! It also requires a continuing commitment to planning and making scrapbooks, to saving and storing important memorabilia, and searching for one's family roots.

Creating a Visual Record
Ask almost anyone what item they would attempt to save from a

159

BUILDING YOUR FAMILY'S FILM RECORD

- Have a family photo taken professionally at least once every year.
- Organize packets of photos and negatives by chronological date in cardboard file boxes.
- Exchange photographs with extended family members to enlarge your collection.
- Buy expandable photo albums with extra pages.
- Give your grandchild an inexpensive camera for taking pictures; develop the film in duplicate.
- Vary settings and locations to maintain interest.
- Keep a camera handy at all times, snapping photos on both a formal and informal basis.
- Read a how-to book as you improve your skills.
- Hold seasonal photo-organizing days accompanied by a delicious dinner.
- Take advantage of disposable cameras: purchase one for each family member on special occasions.
- Take a continuing education class in photography or home video production.
- Encourage friends to send recent photos at Christmastime and do the same for them.

burning house and the answer is often their family's photographs. A number of good reasons lie behind this predictable response, the most obvious one being that most families' photos cannot be replaced.

Photographs, family movies, and videos depict significant milestones: Baby's first steps, successive birthday parties, award ceremonies, concert recitals, a championship basketball game, graduation day. They also capture intimate moments, like the picture I recently saw in our local newspaper of a ninety-two-year-old great-grandmother gently holding her granddaughter's newborn son.

Looking at ourselves through the lens of the camera can make us laugh or cry, depending on what we see. Family pictures allow us to capture glimpses of life that mellow with age. The visual record you create for your family is an invaluable archive—a repository of stored memories. How do you want to approach creating it? As an attentive family historian—with an eye for detail and a certain degree of expertise—or as a casual observer, without paying much attention to the outcome?

If what you have in mind is making a permanent record to be enjoyed for several generations to come, consider buying a good, affordable camera. Invest in equipment that will not strain your budget and that you will feel comfortable using. Learn all you can about the photo-taking or videotaping process by experimenting with lighting, backgrounds, settings, and portrait composition. Be ready to use your skills on a moment's notice and always be sure you have

- Ask extended family members to make copies of old slides and photos; offer to pay costs.
- Make a calendar and circle picture-taking days with a bright-colored marking pen.
- Don't forget the family pets: include animals in your photo sessions for extra fun.

enough film and extra batteries to avoid last-minute panic attacks.

After your film is developed, carefully store the fruits of your labor until you can put the pictures in frames or photo albums. Label videos as soon as you tape them, using the sticky identification labels that come with the cassette, then organize all of your visual archives chronologically so that you can quickly locate specific photos and tapes. Your children and grandchildren will appreciate your efforts—especially when you have them all over for a "Family Memories" night, complete with popcorn and their favorite beverages, to celebrate the wonder of your lives and relationships.

Memory Albums

Buy or design a combined photo album and scrapbook. Find a sturdy book that will stand the test of time and can be added to later as needed. Your local office supply or stationery store is likely to have the best selection. Buy a book that really appeals to you—if you appreciate the way it works and looks, you will be more likely to use it.

Set aside a special storage place. To assemble your scrapbook periodically, select an easy-to-find location for gathering your family's keepsakes and mementos. This will make it easier for you to store and retrieve important items.

Purchase or make a file box for sorting things you want to save. Ticket stubs, travel brochures, special event programs, menus, and the like can be sorted by dates, type of events, child's name, or whatever system you prefer. Fast-file memorabilia soon after you return from an event or outing. By doing so, you will reduce the likelihood of damage and minimize clutter.

Use a keepsake box for protecting potential scrapbook materials and bulky items. Some things require extra room for safe storage, especially dried flowers and corsages, awards, and grandchildren's artwork. Resealable plastic bags are a great way to preserve these special items. So is framing them. Choose a sturdy storage container, put the bags in it, then store it where you can find and reach it easily.

Design an attractive, and perhaps humorous, title page. Using a permanent marker or pen, inscribe your family's name, the album's starting date, your current address and phone number, and other pertinent information. On the second page, make a list of family members (and, if you like, your pets), accompanied by their individual photos.

Develop a table of contents. Possible categories: Milestones (graduations, weddings, baptisms, etc.); Our Special Memories (touching stories, turning points); Grandma's and/or Grandpa's Favorites (especially amusing anecdotes and funny stories); Our Children's Early Years; Family Trips; Friends and Neighbors; Holiday Happenings; and Grandchildren's Visits.

Keep a separate journal or notebook handy. Record memorable information quickly, before you forget the way it happened. Immediate impressions written down for future reference will be appreciated by later generations and can be added to the album as desired.

Create an autobiographical record. Your life story does not need to be professionally published to warrant its writing. Why not make a book of your own to enable your grandchildren to know you better? Consider any of the following topics fair game:

—Your origins: When and where were you born? Describe your parents, including their ages, personalities, beliefs, backgrounds, jobs, achievements, and interests. Where did you live? What did your home look like? Tell about any siblings and all extended family members— grandparents, aunts, uncles, and cousins.

—Your early years: Who was your best friend? List your favorite toys, books, hobbies, television programs, songs, games, foods, movies, sports, and other recreational interests. Did you have any pets? What did you do on holidays and for summer vacations? Share several stories from among your favorite memories.

Recount highlights of your school experiences, including your preferred subjects, top teachers, extracurricular activities (music, sports, drama, church group, school newspaper, youth group, clubs, volunteer work), and any outstanding achievements and awards you received. What was your first paying job? Discuss the cultural trends that influenced your life—clothing, music, politics, entertainment, etc.

—Your life after high school graduation: Did you go to college or go to work? Where? What did you study or do? Paint a picture of your life during this period, including your friends, interests, activities, roommates, daily routines, travel experiences, and career choices.

—Your marriage: How and where did you meet your spouse? Explain the events leading up to your marriage and the day you were wed: favorite dates, how long you knew each other before you considered the possibility of marriage, the circumstances surrounding your engagement, what the ceremony was like.

Relate a few of your best memories and happiest moments, as well as the things that surprised you about being married. Have you shared common interests? What are/were your favorite activities to do together?

If you have been married more than once, talk about your current spouse and any stepchildren you may have and how your life has changed.

—Your children: Describe when and where they were born and how you felt when you became a parent. What were your children like? Provide a birds' eye view of family life in your household—typical routines, notable vacations, big events, tried-and-true traditions. Focus on your personal impressions as well as the milestones.

—Your faith: When did you start believing in God? Share about becoming a Christian—how it affected your life, when you were baptized, where you have attended church, how often you read the Bible, why you pray. Most important, write about your relationship with Jesus.

—Your career: What led you to enter the career you are in? Narrate a vivid account of your work day and what it is like to be employed in your chosen field or profession.

—Your personal favorites: Make a list of your personal favorites using the following suggestions:

Animals
Artwork and artists
Beverages
Books and authors
Bible passages
Cars
Clothes
Colors
Days of the year
Exercise routines
Fabrics
Films and movie stars
Flowers
Foods
Foreign countries
Games
Historical sites and events
Hobbies
Holiday traditions
Jokes, puns, and riddles
Landmarks and cities
Leisure activities
Magazines
Music and musicians
Nature spots
People
Poems and poets
Plays
Prayers

Quiet places

Quotations

Smells

Songs and singers

Sports and athletes

Television shows

Theme parks

Once you have a good start on your family archive collection, why not develop a library to house your memory books, scrapbooks, photo albums, videotapes, and recipes? Your children and grandchildren will appreciate knowing where to look for family-related records and having access to these items. The library will also encourage your family to actually use the collections you have invested hours in creating for their benefit. If you wish, you may allow family members to temporarily "check out" items for their personal use as long as they promise to return them.

Tracing the Family Trees

Today, it is easier to trace your family's ancestors than ever before. Many books, software programs, and continuing education workshops are now available to assist you in this exciting, eye-opening endeavor. Check your local library or Internet listings for ideas to help you get started. Create two family trees for your grandchild using the chart on the following page, making a separate chart for each grandparent. If your partner is absent, you may still want to fill in his or her side of the tree to show a complete picture of your grandchild's background.

Our Family Tree

_____
Grandchild's Name & Birthplace

Mother's Name & Birthplace	Father's Name & Birthplace
Grandmother's Name & Birthplace	Grandmother's Name & Birthplace
Grandfather's Name & Birthplace	Grandfather's Name & Birthplace
Great-Grandmother's Name & Birthplace	Great-Grandmother's Name & Birthplace
Great-Grandfather's Name & Birthplace	Great-Grandfather's Name & Birthplace
Great-Grandmother's Name & Birthplace	Great-Grandmother's Name & Birthplace
Great-Grandfather's Name & Birthplace	Great-Grandfather's Name & Birthplace

Becoming a Spiritual Nurturer

Your values will make their deepest impression on your grandchildren through the way you live your life. "Both my husband and I grew up in a family where church leaders, school teachers, civic authorities, and elderly people were held in respect, where honesty and integrity were practiced, hard work was honorable, being a good neighbor and sharing with those in need was a way of life, and, most important, the Bible was believed and obeyed as they understood it," shares Iona S. Weaver in *Ideas for Families*. "We have tried to live and pass on these values to our children."[1] As your grandkids watch you go about your daily business, what do they hear and see?

Leading Little Ones Toward God

Love Jesus openly. As the old saying reminds us, "Jesus is the silent Listener to every conversation . . . the unseen Guest at every meal."

Why not bring Him into the open where your grandchildren can get to know Him better? By your words and actions, you can convey your vivid love for the Lord and your continuing reliance on His unseen presence. Talking about Jesus tells others that you believe He is alive and active in your life—not a remote, impersonal Savior. Living out a loving relationship with Christ cannot be contained to Sunday morning services and our private devotions.

"On our own, would any of us come up with the notion of a God who loves and yearns to be loved?" asks author

QUESTIONS FOR REFLECTION

- As you prepare to talk with your grandchildren about God, here are questions for you to think about and answer yourself.
- Do you believe God hears and answers your prayers? Why?
- When did you become a Christian? How old were you? What were the circumstances surrounding your conversion?
- How do you know God loves you?
- Who is Jesus?
- Why do you read the Bible?
- What images of Christ do you see revealed in Scripture?
- How do you know Jesus is real?
- If God is good, why do bad things happen?
- Why do you attend church?
- What reminders of God do you see in His creation?
- Where are your favorite places to go when you want to be alone with your heavenly Father?
- When do you feel closest to Jesus?
- Why do you believe God created the earth and everything in it?
- What does it mean to worship the Lord? Why do people worship Him?

Philip Yancey in *The Jesus I Never Knew*.[2] When we allow ourselves to be loved by God—and become God's beloved in return—we can no more contain our joy than if we had just received a marriage proposal from our dream spouse. Love the Lord as He desires, with your whole being—heart, body, mind, and soul—and your grandchildren's lives will be powerfully touched by Christ's presence.

Express your pleasure in being God's child. When Solomon wrote "a cheerful heart is good medicine" (Proverbs 17:22), he was right: recent research shows that laughter enhances the body's ability to ease pain and promote calm by raising natural secretions of endorphins (opiate-like substances) within the nervous system. Our Creator has made us with an inner capacity—a physiological propensity—for experiencing relief from life's stresses and strains.

Children are our teachers in this respect. With childlike wonder, we behold Christ's majesty, bowing before His throne as we encounter the awesome glory of our King. "Believe me," [Jesus] said, "unless you change your whole outlook and become like little children you will never enter the kingdom of heaven. It is the man who can be as humble as [a] little child who is greatest in the kingdom of Heaven" (Matthew 18:3,4, PH). And in His presence, there is fullness of joy.

Listen and respond to your grandchild's spiritual concerns. Respond as simply and honestly as you can to his queries. Make it clear that when it comes to talking about God, Grandma or Grandpa don't consider children's curiosity strange or stupid. Take a break, sit down, and take time to explain your answers at eye level. If your children hold different beliefs than you do, find out in advance if there are any taboo topics.

Look for God in His creation. Spending time outdoors creates a wealth of opportunities to introduce your grandchildren to God's infinite creativity. Dull-looking caterpillars enter cocoons and emerge as brilliantly colored butterflies; a small seed springs up above the ground and grows to be a towering cornstalk; a tiny tadpole sprouts legs and turns into a toad. Meadowlarks and marigolds can teach big truths to little people. Ask simple questions, such as "Can you tell me something God made in my garden that you like to eat?" or "What do you see sitting up there in the oak tree that God made?" to prompt lively hide-and-seek discussions.

Bibles, Books, and Other Blessings

In years gone by, the Bible was often the only book families could afford to own. Family records—births, marriages, baptisms, and deaths—were duly preserved in the prized volume, which sat in a prominent place in the dining room or parlor. Though many

Americans can now afford to own personal copies of the Bible, God's Word continues to play a central part in Christian families' lives.

Once you have grandchildren, you may want to revive the family Bible tradition. It's a lovely way to preserve history while emphasizing the source of living truth. Our family Bible, given to me by my parents twenty-five years ago, has pressed flowers and herbs, photos, and poems inside of it. Perhaps someday, one of my grandchildren will find these things that I have tucked away between the gilded pages. I like this thought. I find it comforting to reflect on what our Bible will mean to someone who I will not meet this side of heaven, but is still a part of me. This Bible is a valuable piece of the lasting legacy I want to leave behind after I am with the Lord.

Two years ago, after I lost my personal Bible on a trip, I felt a deep sense of loss. I found out that the edition I had used over many years—a leather-bound copy of the New English Bible, bought for me at Westminster Abbey by my mother—is no longer available. The dated comments, prayers, sermon notes, observations, highlighted markings, and tear stains I made in it are gone, never to be recovered. Before this happened, I rarely used our large-print family Bible. Now, I realize what a precious heirloom it will be.

I want grandchildren to know about my love for God's Word. I want them to see me reading it, hear me talking about it, and using examples from it. Sunday services, group studies, and bedroom quiet times are just a few of the ways I use my Bible. Bringing it to the forefront of everyday life is essential to me.

I look forward to the time when Abigail asks me to tell her about Jesus, as my own children often did when they were young. Even though I know that her parents are my granddaughter's main Bible teachers, I will still enjoy sharing with her about my relationship with the Lord, the prayers God has answered, and the ways our heavenly Father has helped and strengthened the family over the years. I strongly believe that my love for the Bible will uniquely open up the pages of Scripture for Abigail—from a grandmother's viewpoint.

"As a father of five and grandfather of seven, I'm convinced that one of our most important jobs as parents, teachers, grandparents and ministers is to help children love the Word of God," explains Dr. Beers, former editor of *Christianity Today*, in *Christian Parenting Answers*. "Lifelong habits of reading the Bible come from a love for the Bible, not from an obligation to read it. If you don't generate that love, the Bible will remain a closed book. But how do we build a love for the Bible in the hearts of our preschoolers?"[3] Here are a few ideas, based on Dr. Beers's suggestions:

Be a role model who loves the Bible. Your example will show your grandchildren what the Bible means to you. It is not necessary to be "preachy" when God's Word is alive in your heart and energizing your entire existence. If you genuinely love the Bible, you will convey that attitude to your grandchildren; if you are bored with it or must struggle to study it, this also will make an impression.

Express your love for the Bible in reading times that are fun, enjoyable, and easy to look forward to. When you read or talk about the Bible with your grandchildren, how do you make the message sound? How you present God's Word has a lasting impact on your family. Bible reading

170

should never be boring!

Select Bible stories geared to your grandchild's age group. In recent years, Christian publishers have produced an abundance of children's Bibles and interesting Bible story materials. Check your local Christian bookstore for

child or grandchild? Is that what I truly believe I am passing on to them?

Reprinted from *Christian Parenting Today,* September/October 1989. Used by permission.

examples and select one with an illustrated text and easy-to-understand language.

Mingle Bible reading with family fun times. "A Bible reading around a campfire, on a fun trip, sitting at a picnic table, or on a hike in the woods will stir more love for the Bible than an enforced time that prevents kids from having fun," says Dr. Beers.[4] Choosing the right moment to share God's Word will kindle interest in how the Bible relates to real life by turning your grandchildren's active imaginations toward living truth.

Prayer: The Priceless Gift

Family life provides countless opportunities for prayer. From the time your grandchild is born, speak words of praise and petition in addition to meal- and bedtime blessings. These will be times to cherish! Your prayer and devotion times will bond your family together. It will also allow you to pass along your values, share your beliefs, and set a lasting example for others to follow. Your grandchild will long remember Grandma and Grandpa's tender prayers.

Praying for protection. Prayers for your grandchildren's protection should start before they are born, even before their conception. Though you do not know them yet, you can begin to pray daily for them. It's only natural to feel concerned about this world's dangers. Life is neither harmless nor predictable. We know that we cannot completely protect our children and grandchildren from injury or affliction, but we want to spare our offspring from unnecessary pain. The best way to do this is by praying for them—thanking the Father for the children He sends us, acknowledging His sovereign design for their lives, submitting petitions for specific requests on our family's behalf. We can pray for our grandchildren's spiritual welfare, physical health, and emotional strength. We can pray for their future mates, families, ministries, and vocations. And, most important, we can pray for their redemption, that they might know Jesus Christ as Lord and Savior.

Our prayers will not always be answered according to our expectations—our children, facing infertility, may choose adoption; the newest addition to the family may be born with a serious birth defect; divorce or death may separate loved ones. We cannot insist that God give us an explicit explanation as to why. "The infinite, personal God has done what our minds cannot grasp," explains Edith Schaeffer in *Affliction*. "If we could understand all that God understands, we would no longer be finite and human."[5] Though we cannot see the whole picture, we can be confident that our faithful, fervent, and frequent prayers are heard and answered by our Father.

Silent intercession: continuous prayer. Have you ever been thankful that you do not need to pray out loud for God to know what you are saying? That you can rest in the assurance that the Holy Spirit helps you in your weakness, interceding on your behalf "with groans that words cannot express"? (Romans 8:26) And that "he who searches our hearts knows the mind of the Spirit, because the Spirit intercedes for the saints in accordance with God's will"? (Romans 8:27)

"God gets down on his knees among us; gets on our level and share himself with us. He does not reside afar off and send us diplomatic messages, he kneels among us," writes Dr. Eugene Peterson in *A Long Obedience in the Same Direction*. "God enters into our need, he anticipates our goals, he 'gets into our skin' and understands us better than we do ourselves."[6] Yielding our lives to prayer is a joyous privilege, isn't it? As grandmothers and grandfathers, we can pray for our grandchildren anytime, any place, as the Holy Spirit leads us to intercede on their behalf.

"Never be afraid to bring the transcendent mysteries of our faith,

Christ's life and death and resurrection, to the help of the humblest and commonest wants," advised nineteenth-century hymn writer Phillips Brooks. This is the best kind of help we can give each little one entrusted to our spiritual nurture and loving care.

Standing in the gap. Trusting God with the future when a child strays from the Shepherd's safe pasture is another way that grandparents can provide timely help. Prayers on the family's behalf make a difference, no matter how hopelessly out-of-hand the situation seems. Pulling our attention away from disappointing behavior and difficult life circumstances, we can turn eyes to the Lord and "stand in the gap," as Ezekiel 22:30 suggests, providing crucial prayer covering on the family's behalf. It may be a matter of days or decades before we see conversion or confession take place. In the meantime, we can cast our anxiety at the foot of the Cross and resolutely leave it there.

"How many mistakes I have made with the children because I was 'fretting'—concerned to the point of worry. And invariably it prompted me to unwise action." Ruth Bell Graham says about her children's wilderness years in *Prodigals and Those Who Love Them.* "But a mother who walks with God knows He only asks her to take care of the possible and to trust Him with the impossible; she does not need to fret."[7]

Will you trust God with your child's situation today?

When Family Beliefs Conflict

Let your wise example to be your lasting witness. Unless your children or grandchildren specifically ask you for your opinion on spiritual matters, do not attempt to directly teach them about God. Use a different route to get across your message instead. "Who is wise and understanding among you? Let him show it by his good life, by deeds done in the humility that comes from wisdom" (James 3:13). For now, your faith will shine most brightly through your gracious and gentle manner—a genuine testimony to Christ's love and transforming power.

Respect your children's boundaries. I know very few families where every child and grandchild believes exactly the same things their parents and grandparents do. There is a range of possibilities in this regard, of course—from the twenty-five-year-old married son with a newborn daughter who announces his plans about joining a different denomination to a middle-aged mother living at a Hindu ashram with her three teenage children.

As parents, we would prefer to not face such challenges. But when they do arise, it is encouraging to remember our Father's example: He never coerces, bullies, forces, shames, or intimidates His children. On the contrary, the Bible reminds us that "the wisdom that comes from heaven is first of all pure; then peace-loving, considerate, submissive, full of mercy and good fruit, impartial and sincere. Peacemakers who sow in peace raise a harvest of righteousness" (James 3:17, 18). Let this be the kind of wisdom that perpetually guides your family relationships.

Practice hospitality. Smiles, good food, and generous hospitality are practical displays of Christ's peace. Sharing what you have with your children and grandchildren makes it difficult to withdraw into judgment or resentment. Your open door will not be quickly forgotten.

Don't exclude your grandchild from your devotions. In other words, be yourself. If family prayers, mealtime blessings, morning devotions, Bible study, praising God at the piano, and/or Sunday services are the norm, by all means, continue with your life. When your grandchildren come for a visit, ask God for wisdom and discernment to guide your decisions.

Grandparenting on Purpose

The special poignancy of the grandparent-grandchild relationship springs, in no small part, from our knowledge that time is passing. As each successive year brings its changing seasons, our lives will continue to carry us through the days God has marked out for us.

We may or may not see our grandchildren grow up, marry, and have children of their own. Someday, we know God will call us home, temporarily separating us from our loved ones. Until then, will we approach life haphazardly, without much thought for where we are heading and what we will leave behind? Or will we walk in dignity, laughing at the days to come, purposely investing our love, talent, time, energy, and resources in our grandchildren?

How blessed we are to have been given this opportunity—to share ourselves with a new generation of God's children! Let us show our thanks with our lives, realizing that there is still much we have to offer to—and receive from—our children's children. "Teach us to number our days aright, that we may gain a heart of wisdom," wrote the Hebrew psalmist (Psalm 90:12). It is an apt word for us today, given the daily stresses and competing social pressures we face. Looking beyond the transient to the eternal, let us realize often how precious these fleeting moments with our grandchildren actually are.

Dr. Kenneth Taylor, translator of *The Living Bible* and founder of Tyndale House Publishers, carries a deep appreciation for God's blessing upon his family over many generations. The father of ten children and grandfather of twenty-seven (at the time his autobiography was published), he ends *My Life: A Guided Tour* with this revealing epilogue:

"Nearly three centuries ago, John Lee gave this dying charge to his children and to all of his descendants. I am one of those descendants, so this charge is for me and my children and grandchildren. And now I pass it on to include you."[8]

John Lee's Charge to the Lee Posterity

I charge my dear Children, that you fear God and keep his Commandments and that you uphold his public worship with diligence and constantly as you can and that you be constant in the duty of secret prayer, twice every day all the days of your lives and all you that become to be heads of families that you be constant in Family Prayer, praying evening and morning with your Families besides your prayer at meal and that you in your Prayers you pray for converting grace for yourselves and others, and that God will show you the Excellency of Christ and cause you to love him and believe in him and show you the evil of sin and make you hate forever and turn from it and that you never give over till you have obtained converting grace from God.

Furthermore, I charge you with that you chuse Death rather than deny Christ in any wise or any degree . . . serve God in the way you was brought up in and avoid all Evil Company lest you be led into a snare and temptation. Also be careful to avoid any Excess in Drinking and all other sin and prophaneness and be always dutiful to your mother and be kind to one another.

This I leave in Charge to all my posterity to the End of the World charging every person of them to keep a copy of this my charge to my children. This is my dying Charge to my children.

John Lee

January 13, 1716

Reading his ancestor's letter of legacy, one cannot help but marvel at the way this notable blessing has affected Dr. Taylor's life.

When you and I are gone, what will we leave behind for our grandchildren and their heirs to remember us by? May we pass a precious heritage on to our descendants that will go beyond our life's seasons—one that will outlast temporary jobs, bank accounts, personal achievements, and possessions!

Notes

Chapter 1

[1]Charmaine L. Ciardi, Cathy Nikkel Orme, and Carolyn Quatrano, *The Magic of Grandparenting* (New York: Henry Holt and Co., 1995), 15.

[2]Arthur Kornhaber, *Between Parents and Grandparents* (New York: St. Martin's Press, 1986), 6.

[3]*Ibid.*, 6–7.

[4]Andrew J. Cherlin and Frank F. Furstenberg Jr., *The New American Grandparent* (Cambridge, MA: Harvard University Press, 1992), 50-51.

Chapter 2

[1]As quoted in the *Mayo Clinic Complete Book of Pregnancy & Baby's First Year*, Robert V. Johnson, editor-in-chief (New York: William Morrow and Co., 1994), 56.

[2]National Center for Health Statistics data, as reported by the American College of Obstetricians and Gynecologists, 1985. The American Medical Association Council on Long Range Planning, "The Future of Obstetrics and Gynecology," *Journal of the American Medical Association*, December 25, 1987, 3548.

[3]Richard W. And Dorothy C. Wertz, *Lying-In: A History of Childbirth in America* (New York: The Free Press), 173.

[4]Donald M. Joy, *Bonding: Relationships in the Image of God* (Waco, TX; Word Books, 1985), 112–113.

Chapter 3

[1]Dan Reeves' interview appeared in "Falling in Love Again,"by Sandra Dillard-Rosen. *The Sunday Denver Post*, Sept. 25, 1988, 10.

[2]Marian Tompson's interview appeared in "The Rebirth of Grandparents," by Diane Mason. *American Baby*, June 1985, 42, 44.

Chapter 4

[1]Tracy Hotchner, *Pregnancy & Childbirth: The Complete Guide for a New Life* (New York: Avon Books, 1984), 533.

[2]Donna Ewy, *Preparation for Parenthood* (New York: Plume Books, 1985), 156.

[3]Data from *The New York Times,* cited in *Understanding Sexuality,* by Kurt and Adelaide Haas (St. Louis: Times Mirror/Mosby College Publishing, 1987), 157.

[4] Hotchner, *Pregnancy & Childbirth: The Complete Guide for a New Life,* 533.

[5] T. Berry Brazelton, *Families: Crisis and Caring* (Reading, MA: Addison-Wesley Publishing Company, 1989), 1.

[6]Jay Belsky, with John Kelly, *The Transition to Parenthood* (New York, Delacourte Press, 1994), 45-47.

[7]Eda LeShan, *Grandparenting in a Changing World* (New York: Newmarket Press, 1993), 18, 28.

[8]Bernardine Heimos, *Creative Grandparenting*, (Franklin Park: IL: La Leche League International, 1977), 2-3.

Chapter 5

[1]Dana Raphael, *The Tender Gift: Breastfeeding* (New York: Schocken Books, 1976), 169.

[2]William and Martha Sears, *The Baby Book: Everything Your Need to Know About Your Baby—From Birth to Age Two* (New York: Little,

Brown and Company, 1994), 60.

[3]Carol Dix, *The New Mother Syndrome: Coping with Postpartum Stress and Depression* (Garden City, NY: Doubleday and Co., 1985) 179.

Chapter 6
[1]Raphael, *The Tender Gift: Breastfeeding* , 170.

Chapter 7
[1]Arthur Kornhaber with Sandra Forsyth, *Grandparent Power!* (New York: Crown Publishers, 1994), 37–38.

[2]*Ibid.*, 41.

[3]*Ibid.*, 37.

[4]Adapted from information contained in *Mothercare New Guide to Pregnancy and Child Care,* Penny Stanway, general editor (New York: Simon & Schuster/A Fireside Book, 1994), 242–245.

[5]Frank Minirth, Paul Meier, and Stephen Arterburn, *The Complete Life Encyclopedia* (Nashville: Thomas Nelson Publishers, 1995), 161.

[6]*Ibid.*, 165.

Chapter 9
[1]Charles E. Hummel, *Tyranny of the Urgent* (Madison, WI: InterVarsity Christian Fellowship, 1967), 4.

[2]Brazelton, *Families: Crisis and Caring* , 40, 42.

[3]*Ibid.*, 43-45. Adapted from a list of Dr. Brazelton's suggestions.

[4]*Ibid.*, 45.

[5]Affirmation ideas are based upon information contained in *Self-Esteem: A Family Affair,* by Jean Illsley Clarke (San Francisco: HarperCollins Publishers, 1978).

[6]Kornhaber, 165.

[7]Vicki Lansky, *Vicki Lansky's Divorce Book for Parents: Helping Children Cope with Divorce and Its Aftermath* (New York: Signet, 1991), 208.

[8]*Ibid.*

[9]Dorothy Weiss Gottlieb, Inez Bellow Gottlieb, and Marjorie A.

Slavin, *What to Do When Your Son or Daughter Divorces* (New York: Bantam Books, 1991), 118.

[10]*Ibid.*, 116.

[11]Ricardo Gándera, "Double Duties," *Austin-American Statesman*, August 21, 1995, B6.

Chapter 10

[1]Nick Stinnett, "Six Qualities That Make a Family Strong," in *Family Building: Six Qualities of a Strong Family* , ed. by George Rekers (Ventura, CA: Regal Books, 1985), 40.

Chapter 11

[1]Phyllis Pellman Good and Merle Good, *Ideas for Families* (Intercourse, PA: Good Books, 1992), 233.

[2]Philip Yancey, *The Jesus I Never Knew* (Grand Rapids, MI: Zondervan Publishing House, 1995), 267.

[3]V. Gilbert Beers, "Learning the Word," in *Christian Parenting Answers,* ed. by Debra Evans (Elgin, IL: Chariot Family Publishing/ Christian Parenting Books, 1994), 369.

[4]*Ibid.*, 370.

[5]Edith Schaeffer, *Affliction* (Old Tappan, NJ: Fleming H.Revell, 1978), 26.

[6]Eugene H. Peterson, *A Long Obedience in the Same Direction: Discipleship in an Instant Society* (Downers Grove, IL: InterVarsity Press, 1980), 185.

[7]Quoted in *Study Guide: Prodigals and Those Who Love Them*, Stephen Griffith and Bill Deckard, (Colorado Springs, CO: Focus on the Family Publishing, 1991), 63.

[8]Kenneth N. Taylor, *My Life: A Guided Tour* (Wheaton, IL: Tyndale House Publishers, 1991), 373–374.

Additional Resources

Labor Partnering: What to Expect

According to veteran childbirth educator Penny Simkin, author of *The Birth Partner: Everything You Need to Know to Help a Woman Through Childbirth*, being a good birth partner requires

—A loving bond and a feeling of responsibility toward the mother

—An understanding and acceptance of the mother's personal preferences and peculiarities, including the things that calm and relax her

—Knowledge of what to expect during the labor and birth: the process of childbirth, common medical procedures and interventions, and non-invasive birthing alternatives

—Familiarity with the emotional aspects of childbirth: the emotional phases of labor and a laboring woman's emotional needs

—Practical information concerning how to aid the mother's comfort in a variety of situations

—Ability to adapt to the mother's changing preferences during labor and allowing the mother's emotional and physical needs to determine how, and how much, you help.

"The peak of pregnancy, the birth of a baby, is an everyday miracle—part of a day's work for the doctor, midwife, or nurse, but a deep and permanent memory for the birthing woman and those who love her and support her," says Simkin. "Your role as the birth partner is to do as much as you can to help make this experience a good memory for her."[1]

By becoming familiar with what to expect and how you can help, you can support and ease your daughter's birth experience, a lasting contribution that she will look back on and remember for years to come.

[1]Penny Simkin, *The Birth Partner: Everything You Need to Know to Help a Woman Through Childbirth* (Boston: The Harvard Common Press, 1989), 31.

Labor & Birth: Looking Ahead

Ideally, there are three phases of your daughter's childbearing experience for you to be involved in as a labor partner: prenatal preparation for labor, the birth itself, and the first few weeks after the baby's arrival.

Since you will be functioning as a birth team member, along with your daughter's husband and their health care providers, it helps if you can participate in preparing for the birth together. If possible:

• Attend several childbirth preparation classes with the expectant couple.

• Tour the place where your grandchild will be born.

• Read several current childbirth books.

• Learn the breathing, relaxation, and pushing techniques your daughter plans to use.

• Acquaint yourself with effective pain-relief measures—back rubs, body positions, focusing techniques—that promote labor comfort.

It will be helpful if you can assist her with relaxation, breathing, and comfort techniques within two contexts: during at-home practice and in labor. Prenatal practice enhances your ability to communicate nonverbally with one another and creates a foundation of cooperation, making labor support easier. In addition, your practices can be a special time when you convey your love and support.

When labor begins, try to stay calm and begin encouraging your daughter to relax from the start by using a calm, supportive manner. Watch for expressions of emotional stress and physical discomfort, and be flexible in determining what comfort measures may be useful. When a technique isn't working or she isn't interested in trying it, use something else instead.

You can effectively evaluate how your daughter is feeling during labor by:

—What she says

—What sounds she makes

—What her facial expressions are

—How she responds to her surroundings

—How she moves her body

—How she shows her feelings

—How she relates to people.

Consider questions such as: Does her back seem to be hurting? Is her breathing raspy? Is she grimacing or irritable? Patiently offer help as needed, remaining calm, quiet, and positive in your outlook.

Your touch and caring attention speak clearly to your daughter—rely on your hands and eyes to convey tenderness, patience, and love. Be prepared for mood swings and stress reactions, realizing that it's perfectly normal for even the most cool, calm, and collected women to express serious doubts about their birthing ability. By remaining calm and reassuring, you can provide a stable, soothing reference point during intense labor contractions.

Easing Labor Discomfort: Symptoms & Relief Measures

SYMPTOM	RELIEF MEASURE SUGGESTIONS
Mood change— caused by fatigue, demands of accelerated pace of labor, and little rest.	Give encouragement and reassurance; stay calm; play her prerecorded music; provide a sense of perspective; remember the Lord's presence; thoughtfully offer assistance.
*Emotional withdrawal—*caused by the inability to take breaks from labor's intense demands	Respect the work of labor; stay positive; express acceptance of her feelings; remain in the room quietly
*Trembling, shaking—*caused by physical exertion and metabolic changes	Gentle, firm, rhythmical stroking; warm blanket; encouragement that symptom will soon subside
*Hot flashes—*caused by increased uterine activity and altered metabolism	Remove most (or all) clothing; protect privacy (close drapes or close window blinds); use cool compresses or washcloths; offer ice chips; lower room temperature, if possible
*Chills, cold extremities—*caused by decreased circulation to hands and feet and/or body; due to the uterus' intense muscular exertion	Clean, warm socks; warmed blanket; add extra clothing (robe, sweater); raise room temperature, if possible
*Dry mouth—*caused by breathing techniques and/or medication	Ice chips; sucker; cool washcloth; cool drink; lip balm; slower breathing, especially between contractions
"I want to give up" attitude— caused by stress, fatigue, pain, shorter rest period between contractions	Pain relief techniques; active support; prayer and praise (silent, or aloud if desired); reassurance and encouragement; perspective—"not much longer"

Cervical discomfort—caused by pressure of baby's head against cervix as it stretches open

Encourage release of muscular tension; suggest a different breathing technique, especially during peaks of contractions

Nausea and/or vomiting—caused by uterine effort and disruption of normal digestive activity

Cool compresses; ice chips, peppermint stick; slow breathing; focal point; position change; suggest antinausea medication, if needed.

Backache—caused by pressure of baby moving through pelvis, uterine activity, and mother's position

See "Coping with Back Pain in Labor" (page 187)

Early urge to push—caused by baby's descent into lower pelvis

Ask birth attendant to check dilation; assist with light breathing with quick puffs during "urge to push."

Rectal pressure—caused by baby's head compressing rectum while passing through the pelvis

Remind mother that it's the baby, not a bowel movement; suggest that she release into the pressure instead of tightening against it; encourage her that the pressure means the baby's birth is getting closer

Pressure below the pubic bone—caused by passage of baby under bone area

Light massage over the pubic bone; warm or cool compresses; position change; reassurance

NOTE: While each of these symptoms is common, a woman rarely experiences all of them.

Coping with Back Pain in Labor

Many women experience periodic backache during labor. Often called "back labor," the pain is caused most often by the baby's position. Side-lying (propped with pillows), sitting (cross-legged or with legs flexed and pillow-propped), kneeling, or a fully supported, all-fours position will help shift the baby's weight away from the mother's back.

When desired, you may also offer to:

Massage the lower back. Try giving a firm low-back massage with steady movements, using cornstarch or oil to reduce skin friction. Ask your daughter where to rub and closely follow her cues as to when, and how firmly, to massage.

Apply counterpressure. If the baby's head is pressed down hard against your daughter's pelvis during contractions, provide counter-pressure, pressing firmly and steadily inward against the pelvis at the place where the baby is pressing outward. Do this with your hand, forearm, or a clean paint roller.

Help her take a warm bath or shower. Sitting in a warm bath helps to alleviate pelvic pressure and soothes tense muscles. Dim the lights to further aid relaxation.

Use thermal stimulation. Many women have been helped by having warm or cold applied to the back and other tense areas during labor. Ideas for warm thermal stimulation include baths or showers, compresses (a slow cooker works great for this purpose), a hot water bottle, heating pad, warmed blanket, Mentholatum, and eucalyptus oil. Cold thermal stimulation techniques include ice packs (either commercial chemical packs or self-sealing bags filled with crushed ice), a hot water bottle filled with ice water, cold compresses soaked in ice water, a spray mist of cool water, or four-inch gauze pads soaked in witch hazel (remove excess liquid prior to application).

Assist pelvic rocking. Some women find that the passive pelvic rock—rocking the pelvis between contractions while it is supported by a labor partner—provides additional pain relief by promoting relaxation of pelvic muscles.

Promoting Labor Progress

Your daughter's labor may get off to a slow start, with intermittent menstrual- or flulike abdominal cramping off and on for twenty-four hours or longer without her labor "kicking into gear." Or she may check into the hospital only to discover that she is dilated to two or three centimeters, then labor for four hours or more with little or no change in the cervix.

If your daughter wishes to stimulate her labor's progress, suggest or try the following:

Relaxation. Encourage her to let the uterus do its work as you help her relax during, and between, contractions.

Slow breathing. Slowing and deepening the breathing level supplies extra oxygen to working muscles and calms the central nervous system.

Quiet environment. Protect her privacy by minimizing disruptions, playing music softly, and turning off overhead lights. Try to keep things quiet for at least thirty minutes.

Warm bath or shower. Suggest that she soak in the tub or stand in the shower for a while to ease physical stress.

Walking. Walking is a fabulous way to stimulate labor. It uses gravity in the mother's favor by getting the baby's head down closer against the cervix, aiding dilation. Sitting upright on a bed or in a chair are also helpful labor positions for this reason.

Professional Doulas

The following list is a partial directory of professional *doulas* in the United States. To find out about whether an appropriate service is available in your daughter's area (and also about new groups and private provider's services), write or call the National Association of Postpartum Care Services (NAPCS), P.O. Box 1020, Edmonds, WA 98020; (206) 672-8011. [Note: This information, based on a list of *doula* services provided by NAPCS, is believed to be accurate at the time it was released. It will be your daughter's responsibility to screen the *doula* she selects before hiring her (verify her training, ask about costs, discuss spiritual concerns, etc.)]

ALABAMA

Mother's Helpers, Kerri Skinner & Kay Shelley, Headland, AL 36345; (205) 639-3889. Area served: southeastern Alabama (Dothan and surrounding areas).

Special Touch Services, Judith C. Whorton, RN, CCE, Gadsden, AL 35901; (205) 549-35901. Area served: Northeastern Alabama (primarily Etowah County).

ALASKA

First Step, Carrie Link, Anchorage, AK 99523; (907) 349-5965. Area served: Anchorage; Matsu Valley; Eagle River; Palmer.

CALIFORNIA

After the Stork, Sandy Hill, Rancho Santa Margarita, CA; (714) 589-4311. Area served: Orange County.

BabyTime Birth Service, Laurie Boswell, Goleta, CA 93117; (805) 967-1514. Area served: Santa Barbara, Goleta, Montecito, Carpinteria; expanding to south: Ventura; north: Lompoc.

The Fourth Trimester, Inc., Mindy Zlotnick, San Francisco, CA; (415) 821-7068. Area served: San Francisco, Alameda, Contra Costa, San Mateo, Santa Clara, Marin, and Sonoma counties.

The First Six Weeks . . . A Doula Service, Linda Jones Mixon,

Pinole, CA 94564; (510) 758-3222. Area served: Alameda, Contra Costa, Marin, and San Francisco counties.

Mother Care, Lynn Metrow, Santa Clarita, CA 91380; (818) 879-8541. Area served: Greater Los Angeles, northern suburbs, Riverside, San Bernardino, and Orange counties.

MotherCare, Laurie Dodge, Santa Cruz, CA 95060; (408) 423-3312. Area served: Monterey, Santa Cruz, and Santa Clara counties.

Motherly Care of San Luis Obispo, Vinnie Melone, San Luis Obispo, CA 93403; (805) 544-6667. Area served: San Luis Obispo County.

The Rhythm of Life, Karla and Jodi Hendrix, Dana Point, CA; (714) 661-0246. Area served: Orange County.

Tendercare, Chris Morley, Valencia, CA 91355 (805) 253-2100. Area served: Greater Los Angeles, Santa Clarita Valley, San Fernando Valley, Canejo Valley, Ventura, San Bernadino, and Orange counties.

COLORADO

Helping Hands Doula Care, Betty Arenson, Littleton, CO 80162-0041; (303) 979-3632. Area served: south, southeast, and southwest Denver.

Maternally Yours, Cindy Main, Lakewood, CO 80215; (303) 462-0711. Area served: Lakewood area.

MotherCare of America Doula Service, Joan Goode and Dorothy Harrison, Denver, CO 80206; (303) 321-3287. Area served: Denver and surrounding area, including Boulder.

MotherSupport, Inc., Jennifer Hankins, Fort Collins, CO 80526; (970) 225-1139. Area served: Fort Collins, Loveland, and Greeley (Windsor, Wellington, and Laporte, if needed).

CONNECTICUT

Handle With Care, Tricia Clarke, Ansonia, CT 06401; (203) 735-1127. Area served: call.

MothersCare, Susan Keeney and Sheila Marley, West Haven, CT 06516; (203) 931-1850. Area served: Fairfield and New Haven counties.

FLORIDA

Birth, Bath and Beyond, Marcy Rodriquez, Ormond Beach, FL 32174-0233; (904) 672-3632. Area served: Volusia County.

MotherCare: Postpartum Care Service, Inc., Martha Stewart, Indialantic, FL 32903; (407) 722-1284. Area served: Brevard and Indian River counties.

Tenth Month, Betsy Kraft Schwartz, Coconut Creek, FL 33066; (305) 968-2399. Area served: Broward and Palm Beach counties.

GEORGIA

MomEase, Inc., Dominique Geer, Atlanta, GA 30328-2673; (404) 804-9842. Area served: metropolitan Atlanta.

What About Mom???, Lisa Miller-Farmer, Atlanta, GA 30377; (404) 521-9134. Area served: metropolitan Atlanta.

ILLINOIS

Dana Mothercare, Karen Laing, Chicago, IL 60610; (312) 266-9241. Area Served: metropolitan Chicago.

MARYLAND

Family Affairs, Inc., Dale P. Clark and Kim Miller, Serven, MD 21144; (410) 721-6517. Area served: middle Maryland–Annapolis area.

MAINE

Seacoast Doulas, Marcia Flinkstrom, BA, ACCE, South Berwick, ME 03908; (207) 384-5315. Area served: call.

MASSACHUSETTS

MotherCare Services, Inc., Joan Singer, Lexington, MA 02173; (617) 863-1333. Area served: Greater Boston metropolitan area.

New Baby Basics, Ruth Stevens, Ware, MA 01082; (413) 967-3635. Area served: central and western Massachusetts.

Postpartum Family Care Services, Grete Viddal, Leverett, MA 01054; (413) 548-9344. Area served: western Massachusetts—the Valley area.

Ruth Boland, Ruth Bolan, RN, MSN, MPH, Marblehead, MA 01945; (call local directory information for phone number). Area served: North Shore and Boston vicinity.

MICHIGAN

Doula Care, Inc., Diane L. Barnes, Eastpointe, MI 48201-2910; (313) 774-7611. Area served: metropolitan Detroit and Ann Arbor.

MotherComfort, L.C., Theresa Bowering and Linda Zigterman, Holland, MI 49423; (616) 396-7749. Area served: western Michigan.

NORTH CAROLINA

After the Baby, Melissa Robbins, Durham, NC 27713; (919) 489-7884. Area served: Durham, Chapel Hill, Raleigh, Hillsborough, Pittsboro, Carrboro.

Mother's Helpers, Inc., Cynthia Foley, Fayetteville, NC 28304; (910) 424-0506. Area served: Fayetteville, Cumberland County.

NEW HAMPSHIRE

Mother to Mother of New Hampshire, Amy Healey, Hillsboro, NH 03244; (603) 478-5620. Area served: central and southern New Hampshire.

Time to Bond, Karen Knapp, Hudson, NH 03051; (603) 880-1673. Area served: Hudson, Nashua, Salem, Litchfield, Merrimack.

NEW JERSEY

Friend of the Family, Inc., Mary Basile Logan, Lebanon, NJ 08833; (908) 236-0859. Area served: tri-state area (PA, NY, NJ).

From Our Hearts to Your Family, Hope Ann Miller, Flemington, NJ 08822; (908) 806-7719.

Home from the Hospital, Kathy Akaezuwa, Belle Mead, NJ 08502; (908) 359-1804. Area served: central New Jersey.

MotherLove, Debra Pascali, Ridgewood, NJ 07675; (201) 358-2703. Area served: north and central New Jersey; Manhattan and Westchester County, NY.

NEW YORK

Beyond Birth, Inc., Marguerite Tirelli, Jefferson Valley, NY 10598; (914) 245-BABY. Area served: Westchester and Putnam counties (NY); Fairfield County (CT).

Birth Renaissance, Beverley Small and Teresa Goetz, New York, NY 10024; (212) 595-8067. Area served: Manhattan and Brooklyn.

In a Family Way, Christina Kealy, New York, NY 10024; (212) 877-8812. Area served: metropolitan New York City.

Maternal Instincts, Dawn Salka, RN, Monroe, NY 10950; (914) 496-8808. Area served: Suffern and Orange County, NY; Vernon, NJ.

Mother Nurture, Inc., Alice Gilgoff, Glen Oaks, NY 11004; (718) 631-BABY. Area served: metropolitan New York City and Long Island.

Mothering Mom, Ann Gentry, Liverpool, NY 13089; (315) 652-9910. Area served: Onondaga County.

NewMother Care, Susan Borell, Hampton Bays, NY 11946; (315) 723-CARE. Area served: Eastern Suffolk County.

Ruth Callahan, Ruth Callahan, New York, NY 10025; (212) 749-6613. Area served: New York City; downtown Brooklyn, Park Slope, and the Bronx.

The Tenth Month, Lisa Fearon, Bronxville, NY 10708; (914) 793-8307. Area served: Westchester County, metropolitan New York City, northern Bronx.

OKLAHOMA

Loving Hands, Inc., Anita Campbell, Mannford, OK 74044; (918) 865-7824. Area served: Tulsa and surrounding area (Broken Arrow, Jenks, Bixby, Sand Springs).

OREGON

Postpartum Care Services, Vicky York, Portland OR 97210; (503) 241-8682. Area served: Portland area:(Multnomah and Washington counties); Vancouver, WA area .

PENNSYLVANIA

Advisors in Baby Care, Kathy B. Schadler, Allentown, PA 18102; (610) 433-4522. Area served: Lehigh Valley area, Allentown, Bethlehem.

Postpartum Pampering, Martha Baker, RN, Corapolis, PA 15108; (412) 331-BABY. Area served: Allegheny County.

SOUTH CAROLINA

Mother's Helper, Lin Cook, Charleston, SC 29407; (803) 776-6135. Area served: Charleston and Mt. Pleasant area.

TENNESSEE

Mother Love, Debbie Felton, Jackson, TN 38301; (800) 530-7401. Area served: call.

TEXAS

Doula Support Service, 3906 S. Lamar, Suite 207, Austin, TX 78756; (512) 371-0782. Area served: call.

Family Care, LaVerne Campbell, Fort Worth, TX 76140; (817) 568-0696. Area served: Tarrant County; Fort Worth.

Mother-To-Mother Postpartum Care Service, Nancy J. Mowry, Plano, TX 75023; (618) 618-1252. Area served: north Dallas suburbs and Plano.

VIRGINIA

Adopt-A-Doula, Janet Francisco, Manassas, VA 22110-7213; (703) 361-7078. Area served: northern Virginia.

Mother's Matters, Inc., Gerri Levrini, RN, MSN, Reston, VA 22091; (703) 620-3323. Area served: Virginia; Maryland; metropolitan Washington, D.C.

Tidewater Postpartum Care, Larissa Blechman, Virginia Beach, VA 23462; (804) 490-7596. Area served: Virginia Beach, Norfolk, Portsmouth, Chesapeake, Newport News, Hampton, and York.

WASHINGTON

MotherCare of America Doula Service, Dorothy Harrison, Edmonds, WA 98020 (206) 672-8011. Area served: Greater Seattle metropolitan area, including King and Snokomish counties, parts of Pierce county, Gig Harbor, Bellevue, and Issaquah.

WISCONSIN

After the Stork, E. Burnett and D. Gallagher, De Pere, WI 54115; (414) 336-6378. Area served: Greater Green Bay area.

CANADA

Post Natal Helpers, Ltd., Lynn Gilmour, Calgary, Alberta T3C 3P6, Canada; (403) 640-0844. Area served: Calgary and surrounding communities.

Baker's Dozen of Balanced Personal Snacks for Mom

Fruit 'n' Nuts Yogurt

Stir together and serve in a small bowl:

1/2 cup vanilla yogurt

1 small apple, cored and chopped

4 walnut halves, chopped

sprinkle of cinnamon

OJ Crush

Put the following ingredients in a blender with 4-6 ice cubes; blend until ice is crushed.

1 6 oz. can frozen orange juice

1 6 oz. can water

1/3 cup nonfat dry milk powder

1/2 teaspoon vanilla extract

Strawberry Crush

Put the following ingredients in a blender; blend until smooth (about 30 seconds).

1 cup skim or low fat milk

1/2 cup unsweetened frozen strawberries, partially thawed

1/2 teaspoon sugar

1/2 teaspoon vanilla

Muffin Moment

Bran muffin; orange sections; glass of milk

Potato Pleaser

Baked potato with a selection of toppings served on the side; glass of milk

Pizza Muffin

1/2 English muffin

1 tablespoon pizza sauce

1–2 ounces shredded mozzarella cheese
Choice of toppings: ham, mushrooms, spinach, pepperoni, green pepper, feta cheese, etc.
Place under broiler until cheese melts or microwave on high for about 35–40 seconds.

Bagel Plus

Toasted bagel topped with cream cheese; 10 toasted almonds; fresh pear

PB, No J

4-6 whole wheat crackers spread with peanut butter; 1/2 grapefruit; glass of herbal iced tea

Yogurt Break

8 oz. carton vanilla, lemon, or coffee-flavored yogurt; 2 graham crackers; Spanish peanuts; iced or hot tea (decaffeinated)

Bread & Spread

1 slice cinnamon-raisin bread spread with lemon curd (or favorite preserves);1 cup fresh strawberries, blackberries, or raspberries; glass of milk

Chicken Snack

Chicken strips, seasoned and cooked; 2–3 cups air-popped popcorn; 1 cup seedless grapes

Veggie Snack

Carrot and celery sticks; low-fat sour cream dip; 1 hard-boiled egg; glass of sparkling fruit juice

Fruit Snack

1/2 cup creamed cottage cheese; 2 pineapple slices or pear halves; Ry-Krisp or melba toast

Grab-and-Go Snacks

- Cheese and crackers
- Rice cakes
- Whole-grain cereal and milk
- Frozen bagels and English muffins with reduced-fat, flavored cream cheese spread
- Fresh fruit: apples, grapes, bananas, pears, oranges, etc.
- Cottage cheese
- Low-sodium pretzels
- "Lite" microwave popcorn
- Veggies-in-a-bag: salad mix, carrots, broccoli flowerettes, celery hearts, etc.
- Reduced-fat granola bars
- Low-fat, whole grain, high-fiber muffins
- Roasted peanuts (fresh from the shell)
- Dried fruit: apricots, apples, raisins
- Instant pudding
- Angel food cake
- Frozen fruit bar

The First-aid Kit

- acetaminophen (Tylenol, Tempra, Liquiprin, or other reliable brand) pain reliever: tablets, liquid, or suppositories
- adhesive tape (1 inch) to hold bandages in place
- alcohol swabs
- antibiotic cream or ointment
- antiseptic cleansing solution (Hibiclens, Betadine, etc.)
- assorted bandages: Steri-strips or butterfly adhesive bandages for closing small cuts; gauze squares (3 and 4 inch sterile, single-wrapped)
- bandage wrap: "quick" wrap or gauze bandages (1 and 2 inch) to apply nonstick pads; nonstick pads; self-stick adhesive bandages in several sizes
- baking soda: use as paste to relieve itching, bug stings, heat rash
- cotton balls or pads; cotton-tip applicators (Q-tips)
- eye cup and eye-cleansing solution
- first-aid instruction manual
- flashlight
- heating pad to ease discomfort from stomach cramps, chills
- hydrocortisone cream (0.5%) for relief of itching, stings, eczema
- hydrogen peroxide (3% solution) to clean wounds
- instant ice packs to reduce pain and swelling from bumps and insect bites
- lubricating jelly (water soluble) for rectal thermometer
- magnifying glass
- medication measuring dropper and measuring spoon
- nasal syringe for clearing mucus from baby's nose, especially before feeding
- pad of paper and a pen or pencil
- picture books
- scissors with rounded tips to cut bandages
- syrup of ipecac to induce vomiting in case of poisoning

Note: Use as directed only after phoning physician or poison control

- thermometer (rectal and/or oral, depending on child's age; glass or digital)
- toys and other treats
- tweezers to remove splinters

Poisonous Plants

Akee
Almond tree
Aloe
Amaryllis bulbs
Angel's trumpet
Apple tree, seeds
Apricot tree
Autumn crocus
Azalea
Baneberry
Balsam pear
Beach apples
Belladonna lily
Bittersweet
Bleeding Heart
Bloodroot
Buttercup
Caladium
Cashew
Castor beans
Cherry tree
Chinaberry tree
Christmas pepper
Christmas rose
Comfrey
Cowitch
Cow's horn
Cowslip
Creeping spurge
Crown of thorns
Daffodil bulbs
Daphne
Death camas
Delphinium
Dieffenbachia (dumbcane)
Elderberry

Elephant ear
English holly
English ivy
False hellebore
Foxglove (digitalis)
Gingko berries
Glory lily
Golden chain tree
Holly
Horse chestnuts
Hyacinth bulb
Hydrangea
Iris bulbs
Jack-in-the-pulpit
Jasmine
Jerusalem cherry
Jimson weed
Jonquil bulbs
Lady's slipper
Lantana
Larkspur
Lily of the valley
Locust tree
Lupine
Mace (check quantity)
Mayapple
Milkweed
Mistletoe
Monkshood root
Moonseed
Morning glory
Mountain laurel
Mushrooms (check quantity)
Narcissus bulbs
Nettle
Nicotiana

Nightshade
Nutmeg (check quantity)
Oak tree, acorns
Oleander
Peach tree
Peyote
Philodendron
Poinsettia
Poison hemlock
Poison ivy
Poison oak
Poison sumac
Pokeweed
Potato plant leaves
Pothos
Primrose
Privet
Rhododendron
Rhubarb plant leaves
Rosary pea seeds
Sandbox tree
Sassafras
Skunk cabbage
Snakeroot
Sneezeweed
Snowdrop bulbs
Snow-on-the-mountain
Spider lily
Sweet pea seeds
Tapioca plant
Tobacco
Tomato leaves
Virginia creeper
Water hemlock
Wisteria seeds
Yew

Poisonous Substances

- Acids, lye, and other caustics
- Alcoholic drinks and beverage containers
- Benzene
- Bleach products, stain removers, fabric softeners, and some detergents
- Bubble bath
- Car products: antifreeze, window wash solvents, and petroleum products
- Cleaning fluids and compounds: oven cleaner, ammonia, etc.
- Corn and wart removers
- Cosmetics and perfumes
- Dishwashing detergent and rinse agents
- Disinfectants and pine oil
- Drain and toilet bowl cleaners
- Flammable liquids: lighter fluid, gasoline, kerosene, lamp oil, etc.
- Flavoring extracts (vanilla, almond, orange, etc.)
- Furniture polish and wax
- Glue, solvents, and model cement
- Hair products: shampoo, perm and color solutions, straighteners, etc.
- Ink, pens, markers, typewriter cleaner, and correction fluid
- Insect sprays and bug traps
- Iodine and rubbing alcohol
- Lawn and garden products: pesticides, fertilizers, snail bait, etc.
- Leather cleaner, shoe polish, and suede spray
- Medicated ointments, creams, and oils
- Medicated powders, especially those with boric acid
- Moth crystals, flakes, and cakes
- Mouse and rat poisons
- Mouthwash
- Nail polish and remover
- Paint, varnish, turpentine, paint thinner, and woodworking products

- Pet sprays, medicines, shampoos, and flea treatments
- Poisonous plants
- Prescription and over-the-counter drugs
- Room deodorizers
- Salt
- Shaving cream, cologne, and aftershaves
- Silver, copper, and brass polish
- Suntan products
- Tobacco products
- Vitamin and mineral supplements
- Water softeners

Postpartum Information And Support

International Childbirth Education Association (ICEA), P.O. Box 20048, Minneapolis, MN 55420; (612) 854-8660. Founded in 1960, ICEA offers referrals to local groups sponsoring grandparenting classes. Also available free from this nonprofit association: bookmarks, a catalog of books, pamphlets, and videotapes concerning all aspects of family-centered childbearing, breast-feeding, postpartum support, and newborn care. To order, call (800) 624-4934.

National Association of Postpartum Care Services (NAPCS), P.O. Box 1020, Edmonds, WA 98020; (206) 672-8011. NAPCS offers information on *doula* services in North America, including information about members who provide direct care to women during birth and the postpartum period.

Depression After Delivery (DAD), P.O. Box 1282, Morrisville, PA 19067. (215) 295-3994. With more than eighty groups nation-wide, this nonprofit, peer support organization offers referrals to local chapters and professional services. It will also send you a free information packet on request. If no group exists in your area, you will be given a list of DAD-approved phone contacts. The group is made up of women who have experienced postpartum depression and belong to a group in their community; local professionals attend meetings. A quarterly newsletter is included in the basic membership fee, but membership isn't required to obtain support.

Breastfeeding National Network, Medela, Inc., P.O. Box 660, McHenry, IL 60051-0660;(800) TELL-YOU. This telephone service, provided without charge by Medela, a breast pump manufacturer, gives pre-recorded local pump and rental information (as well as descriptions of breastfeeding services and referrals to lactation consultants in your area) when you punch in your Zip Code.

International Lactation Consultant Association (ILCA), 1400 North Meacham Road, P.O. Box 4079, Schaumburg, IL 60168-4079; (800) 525-3243. Breastfeeding specialists receive board certification as lactation consultants through this international organization. Clinical practice, continuing-education credit, and an extensive exam are required. ILCA will refer you to an IBCLC (International Board Certified Lactation Consultant) in your area for expert breast-feeding support and assistance.

La Leche League, P.O. Box 1209, 9616 Minneapolis Ave., Franklin Park, IL 60131-8209; (800) LA-LECHE. The oldest peer support group in the United States, this nonprofit group continues to provide these services across the world: mother-to-mother breast-feeding phone helplines; support and education through local group meetings; peer group support in inner-city clinics and hospitals; professional workshops for lactation consultants (LCs), nurses, midwives, and physicians; publication of a bimonthly members' magazine, *New Beginnings*, a catalog of books, pamphlets and products; and its 800 number for referrals to certified LLL leaders around the country.

Free Information

Amercian Academy of Pediatrics, P.O. Box 927, Elk Grove Village, IL 60009-0927. A list of free baby and child care brochures is available on request; send a business-size self-addressed, stamped envelope to receive a copy.

Association for Childhood Education International, 11501 Georgia Avenue, Suite 315, Wheaton, MD 20902; (800) 423-3563. Provides free information on a child's first year of development.

Consumer Information Catalog, P.O. Box 100, Pueblo, CO 81002. Offers numerous pamphlets, brochures, and booklets for little or no cost.

Safety Concerns and Baby-proofing Products

U.S. Consumer Product Safety Commission. A free catalog of current no-cost publications about the safety of consumer products is yours for the asking. For immediate assistance regarding the safety of baby and child products, call (800) 638-2772.

National Highway Traffic Safety Administration Auto Safety Hotline: (800) 424-9393. Questions concerning car seat safety? Obtain up-to-the-minute information from NHTSA's toll-free hotline.

Assorted child safety products. The following safety items (and more) may be ordered over the phone from the following companies: Playskool, (800) PLAYSKL—Super Corner Guards (four for under $2) and Cabinet Lock ($2); Gerber, (800)-4-GERBER—Invisible Outlet Plugs (12 for under $2), Door Knob Cover and Lock Guard (two for under $2); Fisher-Price/Mericon, (800)-753-SAFE—Safe-Plate electrical outlet cover ($3.50) Perfectly Safe, (800) 837-KIDS— Window Guards ($15 to $25, price varies by size); The First Years, (800) 533-6708—Ipecac Medi-Pack ($5) and Double Guard Cabinet and Door Lock (two for $4).

Grandparent Advocacy Books, Groups, and Organizations

Grandchildren Visitation Disputes: A Legal Resource Manual. Available for $19.95, plus $2.95 postage and handling, from American Bar Association Fulfillment, 750 Lakeshore Drive, Chicago, IL 60611.

Intergenerational Handbook. Available for $22.50 from the Intergenerational Activities Program, Broome County Child Development Council, 29 Fayette Street, P.O. Box 880, Binghampton, NY 13902-0880.

Grandparents-Grandchildren: The Vital Connection. Available for $18.85 from Dr. Arthur Kornhaber, 12 Sheldon Road, Cohasset, MA 02025.

Grandparent's-Grandchildren's Rights, Lee and Lucille Sumpter, 5728 Bayonne, Haslett, MI 48840.

Grandchildren's Rights to Grandparents, 237 S. Catherine, La Grange, IL 60525.

Grandparent's Rights Organization, Richard S. Victor, 555 S. Woodward Ave., Suite 600, Birmingham, MI 48009.

The National Grandparent Information Center, Social Outreach and Support Center, 601 E. Street, N.W., Washington, D.C. 20049.

ROCKING (Raising Our Children's Kids), Box 96, Niles, MI 49120.

Grandparents Raising Grandchildren (GAP), Barbara Kirkland, P.O. Box 104, Colleyville, TX 76034.

Grandparents' Programs and Newsletters

Groups and individuals marked with an asterisk (*) will send a sample newsletter if you send them a stamped (fifty-five cents), self-addressed, 8" X 11" envelope. Otherwise, to obtain information, simply send a stamped (thirty-two cents), self-addressed business-sized envelope, along with your inquiry, to obtain more information about a particular person or organization.

Creative Grandparenting*, Robert Kasey, 609 Blackgates Road, Wilmington, DE 19803. Positive grandparenting through the sponsorship of various projects, including an innovative "grandparents as mentors" program, is this group's primary goal.

Foundation for Grandparenting*, Arthur Kornhaber, M.D., Box 326, Cohasset, MA 02025. Dedicated to promoting the importance of grandparents and grandparenting activities for the betterment of children, families, and society, this non-profit organization publishes a quarterly newsletter, participates in intergenerational research (in conjunction with the St. Francis Academy), operates a summer camp for grandparents and grandchildren, and sponsors national grand-parenting conferences.

Grandparent Classes: Becoming a Better Grandparent, Shirley and Robert Strom, College of Education, Arizona State University, Tempe, AZ 85287-0611.

"Grandparenting Little Dividends" Young Grandparents Clubs*, Sunie Levin, P.O. Box 1143, Shawneee Mission, KS 66207-1143. Newsletter is loaded with good grandparenting tips; information about groups in your area is available by SASE request.

The Joy of Grandparenting, Clarice A. Orr, 7100 Old Post Rd. #20, Lincoln, NE 68506. Send your name and address to obtain information on this organization's nationwide network of effective grandparenting classes.

National Federation of Grandmothers Clubs of America, 203 N. Wabash Ave., Chicago, IL 60601. As the oldest existing grandparent organization in the United States, this assocation and its members devote themselves primarily to volunteer and charitable activties.

"Too Far Away Grandparents Newsletter"*, Mike Moldovan, P.O. Box 71, Del Mar, CA 92014. Practical tips on staying in touch with your grandchildren are the main focus of this newsletter.

Games for Travelers

Trouble-Free Travel with Children: Helpful Hints for Parents on the Go, Vicki Lansky (The Book Peddlers, 1991); 156 pages. Handy tips on family travel, ranging from packing checklist to medical hints, are provided in this helpful paperback.

Travel Games for Kids! Andrew Langley (Berkshire House, 1992); 108 pages. Gives more than one hundred fun game ideas for children ages four to fourteen, including hand games, puzzles, and word play.

Miles of Smiles, Carole Terwilliger Meyers (Carousel Press, 1993); 123 pages. Loaded with entertaining en route activities to amuse children ages four and up.

Are We There Yet? Travel Games for Kids, Richard Salter (Crown, 1991). 90 pages. Fifty creative travel games requiring only a pencil, a piece of paper, and a watchful eye for identifying numbers, letters, and signs, for children six years and up.

Recommended Reading

Baby and Child Medical Care, ed. Terril H. Hart (Meadowbrook Press, 1992).

The Baby Book: Everything You Need to Know About Your Baby—From Birth to Age Five, William and Martha Sears (Little, Brown, 1993).

Between Parents and Grandparents, Arthur Kornhaber (St. Martin's, 1986).

The Christmas Book, Alice Slaikeu Lawhead (Shaw, 1990).

The Complete Life Encyclopedia, Frank Minirth, Paul Meier, and Stephen Arterburn (Nelson, 1995).

Crying Babies, Sleepless Nights, Sandy Jones (Harvard Common Press, 1992).

Finding Dollars for Family Fun, Gwen Weising (Revell, 1993).

First Aid for Children Fast, Johns Hopkins Children's Center (Dorling Kindersley, 1995).

Grandmother Remembers: A Written Heirloom for My Grandchild, Judith Levy (Stewart, Tabori, and Chang, 1983).

Grandparent Power!, Arthur Kornhaber with Sandra Forsyth (Crown, 1994).

Ideas for Families, Phyllis Pellman Good and Merle Good (Good Books, 1992).

Living More with Less, Doris Janzen Longacre (Herald Press, 1980).

Loaves and Fishes: A "Love Your Neighbor" Cookbook, Linda Hunt, Marianne Frase, and Doris Liebert (Herald Press, 1980).

More-with-Less Cookbook, Doris Janzen Longacre (Herald Press, 1976).

A Sigh of Relief: The First-Aid Handbook for Childhood Emergencies, Martin I. Green (Bantam, 1994).

What Is a Family? Edith Schaeffer (Revell, 1975).

Looking for the perfect gift for your grandchild?
How about these best-selling Bible storybooks from
Chariot Victor Publishing?

The Baby Bible Storybook
by Robin Currie
ISBN: 0-78140-076-7
Retail: $11.99

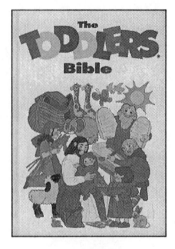

he Toddlers Bible
by V. Gilbert Beers
ISBN: 0-89693-077-7
Retail: $16.99

The Children's Discovery Bible
taken from David C. Cook's
Primary Curriculum

ISBN: 0-78141-546-2
Retail: $17.99